Sharpen Your Bridge Technique:

How to Think Like an Expert

HUGH KELSEY

LONDON
VICTOR GOLLANCZ LTD
in association with
Peter Crawley
1988

First published in 1981 by
Faber & Faber Ltd

First paperback edition published in 1988
in association with Peter Crawley
by Victor Gollancz Ltd
14 Henrietta Street,
London WC2E 8QJ

British Library Cataloguing in Publication Data
Kelsey, H.W. (Hugh Walter)
   [Bridge]. Sharpen your bridge technique:
   how to think like an expert.——(Master
   bridge series).
   1. Contract bridge. Card play – Manuals
   I. [Bridge]   II. Title   III. Series
   795.41'53

ISBN 0-575-04186-2

Printed in Great Britain by WBC Print Ltd, Bristol.

Acknowledgements

Again I am grateful to Denis Young, whose criticism of the manuscript has persuaded me to keep my feet, if not exactly on the ground, at least closer to the ground than they would otherwise have been.

H. W. K.

Contents

INTRODUCTION

Expertise in the play of the cards is a recognizable quality although, paradoxically, it may pass unnoticed in an average bridge game. As a general rule it takes an expert to appreciate expert technique, which can be so far removed from the practice of the average player as to be totally incomprehensible to him. It follows that in attempting to lay bare the secrets of the expert mind I am taking on an ambitious task—some might say an impossible one.

Anyway, is there really such a thing as 'the expert mind'? Is not each expert an individual with his own particular strengths and weaknesses, brilliant in some aspects of card play but less sure of his mastery in others?

It is true in a sense that the champions are all different. Some delight in psychological coups, for instance, while others prefer to rely on reasoned analysis. Yet in many ways the experts are all the same. In learning to take account of many factors that simply would not occur to the average player, they have developed certain patterns of thought that set them apart in a class of their own. It is by examining those patterns of thought that we can hope to penetrate the mind of the expert and discover what the game is like at his level. Quite simply, to become an expert you have to think like an expert.

Is the exercise worth while? When you have read this book I believe you will agree that it is. Bridge is a game that can give pleasure at many different levels. The better you play the more you enjoy the game, and the rewards are not confined to the joy of winning although it is always gratifying to win. The pleasure at expert level comes in equal measure from a heightened awareness of the intricate structure of cards, from the ability in one sphere of activity to produce order out of chaos, and from an occasional glimpse of metaphysical delights that are normally hidden from the eyes of men.

Chapter 1

CARD SENSE

A bridge expert can be described in simple terms as a player who makes fewer mistakes than most. What we have to do, clearly, is to seek out the reasons why he makes fewer mistakes. There are a couple of qualities in particular without which no player can hope to become an expert. The first of these is what is known as 'card sense'.

A certain mystique and a great deal of muddled thinking surround this term, which has never been adequately defined. Some claim that card sense is a gift of nature—an endowment that you have to be born with—while others contend that it is something that can be acquired by diligent practice. Discussion is hardly possible unless we clarify our terms, and it seems to me that all difficulties are resolved if we accept the definition of card sense as 'a natural aptitude for card play'. In that case card sense *is* a gift of the gods. Just as a person with a natural aptitude for ball games—'a good eye for a ball'—is likely to excel at tennis, football or squash, someone born with a natural aptitude for cards is destined to succeed at bridge. Most bridge players *do* possess card sense to a greater or lesser degree. That is what led them to discover their affinity for the game in the first place.

The presence or absence of card sense in the make-up of an individual is in no way a measure of general intelligence. Many people who are quite brilliant in their own fields play an indifferent game of bridge and are never likely to show any great improvement. A player deficient in card sense can compensate to some extent by working hard at the game, but he cannot expect to achieve more than moderate success.

Can we arrive at any firm conclusions about the nature of this elusive quality that we call card sense? Obviously it is a function of the mind even if it is not directly related to brain power. Some form of intelligence must lie at the root of it, although not necessarily intelligence of a high order.

Success at bridge appears, in fact, to require a certain type of mind—a mind capable of assembling a wide range of data, analysing it and drawing the correct conclusions. It is the type of mind possessed by crossword enthusiasts, puzzle solvers and cipher experts. Bridge is above all an analytical game.

Confirmation of this theory is found if we examine how the top exponents of the game earn their bread. Few can rely on bridge for a living. Most of the experts have to work, and a surprising number of them are employed in the computer industry as programmers or systems analysts, jobs where they utilize the same skills that they bring to the bridge table. Thus there would seem to be a marked relationship between computer aptitude and card sense. Also well represented in the ranks of the experts are lawyers, doctors and teachers, all professions in which logical analysis is to the fore. There appears to be no special affinity between bridge and mathematics. This is not really surprising since it does not take a mathematical genius to add up to thirteen. There are perhaps as many musicians as mathematicians at the top level. The rest of the experts are drawn from a wide variety of backgrounds, but they all have this attribute in common—the analytical turn of mind which can loosely be described as card sense.

In the expert, card sense is developed to an unusually high degree. Analytical power increases with use, and experience is a great asset. In most situations at the bridge table the expert has the advantage of having 'been there before'. From the vast backlog of bridge hands stored in his memory he can usually retrieve at least one that is relevant to the problem that he faces and apply the appropriate remedy.

Here is a simple problem to test your card sense.

           ♠ 10 6 5
           ♡ K 8 5
           ◇ 10 6 5 3 2
           ♣ K 3

           ♠ Q 2
           ♡ Q J 7 4 2
Game all.   ◇ A K
Dealer South.   ♣ J 7 6 2

South	West	North	East
1♡	pass	2♡	pass
pass	pass		

West leads the three of hearts to the five, nine and queen. How do you plan the play?

Prospects are poor. Clearly you must hope to find West with the ace of clubs, and it seems natural to play a club at trick two in an attempt to score at least one club ruff in dummy. However, your card sense is not functioning properly if you are thinking along those lines. The defenders have already started their attack on your trumps and it is too late to hope for a club ruff on the table. Two further rounds of trumps will be played as soon as an opponent gains the lead and then, unless you are lucky enough to find West with exactly A Q x in clubs, you will have to lose three clubs, two spades and a trump.

Danish expert Stig Werdelin was faced with this problem when partnering Steen Moller in the *Sunday Times* Invitation Pairs of 1978. The defenders were the formidable Italians, Belladonna and Garozzo. Werdelin's highly-developed card sense warned him of the futility of an immediate club lead and suggested an effective counter to the threatening trump leads. He simply cashed the ace and king of diamonds before playing a club. Here is the complete deal.

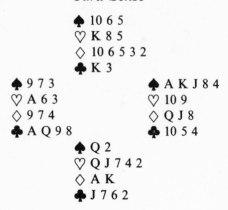

♠ 10 6 5
♡ K 8 5
◇ 10 6 5 3 2
♣ K 3

♠ 9 7 3   ♠ A K J 8 4
♡ A 6 3   ♡ 10 9
◇ 9 7 4   ◇ Q J 8
♣ A Q 9 8   ♣ 10 5 4

♠ Q 2
♡ Q J 7 4 2
◇ A K
♣ J 7 6 2

When the king of clubs won at trick four, Werdelin was able to ruff a diamond, establishing two diamond winners on the table. Now there was no defence when he continued with a second club. If the defenders played the ace and another heart, declarer would be in a position to take nine tricks by discarding two of his black losers on the diamonds. The best the defence could do was to cash the ace of hearts and then force dummy with a third round of clubs, but that was still eight tricks for South.

Werdelin would not have scored badly if he had gone one down in two hearts, since East and West could have made two spades. Making two hearts gave an excellent score, of course.

Note the essential simplicity of Werdelin's play. It was just a matter of unblocking the diamonds so as to be in a position to take advantage of a 3–3 break in the suit. But how many players would have thought of it? Werdelin thought of it because experts have a habit of thinking of things like that.

To his well-developed card sense the expert adds the qualities of vision and imagination, which enable him to foresee the likely course of events on many hands and take steps where necessary to divert them. Test your card sense again with this defensive problem.

♠ 10 9 6 4
♡ J 10 8 6
◇ 10 6 3
♣ 7 3

♠ 8 5 2
♡ K 7 5
◇ Q J 9 8 7   E-W game.
♣ A 10   Dealer South.

South	*West*	*North*	*East*
2♣	pass	2◇	pass
3NT	pass	pass	pass

After this uninformative auction you lead the queen of diamonds. Partner plays the four and declarer wins with the king. South cashes the ace of spades, East playing the three, and continues with the queen of spades which East wins with the king. The four of clubs is returned to South's king and your ace. What now?

Let's have an instant reaction without going too deeply into the position. Do you feel an overwhelming urge to follow a particular line of defence?

I believe that any defender with a keenly developed card sense should feel a compulsion to return a low diamond at this point, even if the reasons are not consciously understood. The need for this defence can in fact be deduced from the available data. Why didn't partner return a diamond instead of a club? It can only be because he does not have one, so you can place declarer with A K 5 2 in the suit. Partner's lead of the four of clubs indicates that declarer must also have four cards in that suit. From the play of the spades South is marked with A Q J, which means that he can have only two hearts.

It is not strictly relevant to the problem, but if South is a good player you can be sure that his hearts will be A x and not A Q, for with the latter holding he would have tackled hearts instead of spades at trick two. It follows that partner would have defeated the contract rather more easily by returning a heart instead of a club. And declarer is a point short for his bid, even if he has K Q J in clubs. Since we know the complete picture we may as well set out all four hands.

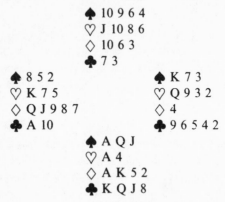

The danger is clear. Dummy's fourth spade will provide the ninth trick for declarer if he is permitted to score it. On a neutral return such as the ten of clubs South will win, unblock the jack of spades and play a low diamond, eventually gaining access to dummy with the ten of diamonds to cash the last spade. To be sure, you can harry his communications a little by rising with the jack of diamonds and switching to hearts, but whether you play a small heart or the king declarer can still get home.

You avoid all danger by returning a low diamond at trick five. Declarer is forced to use the ten of diamonds at a time inconvenient to him—before the spades are unblocked.

Does it mean that you are lacking in card sense if you failed to see the need for a diamond return? Not at all, but it does perhaps indicate that your card sense is in need of further development. In difficult defensive problems of this sort even experts go wrong. Two experts did get it wrong, in fact, when the hand was played in the 1957 Bermuda Bowl contest between the U.S.A. and Italy, the contract of three no trumps being allowed to make in both rooms.

These defensive problems can be hard work. Try another hand as declarer.

```
               ♠ Q 8 4 2
               ♡ A
               ◇ Q 4
               ♣ K 9 8 5 4 2

               ♠ A 6
               ♡ J 8 6 2
N–S game.      ◇ A K J 10 9 6 3
Dealer West.   ♣ —
```

West	North	East	South
2◇*	pass	2♡	3NT
pass	4♣	pass	5◇
pass	6◇	dble	pass
pass	pass		

* Multi, in this case a weak two bid in a major.

After a somewhat eccentric bidding sequence you play in six diamonds, and West leads the three of clubs in response to his partner's double. When you play low from dummy East puts in the queen. How do you play?

At least you can be thankful that they didn't lead a trump. Naturally you will ruff the first trick, but unless your card sense tells you to ruff with the six of diamonds and not the three you will have thrown away your best chance of making the slam. The urge to ruff high should be instinctive, although there are sound enough reasons for the move.

Clearly West's suit must be hearts, for with long hearts and short spades East's response would have been two spades. You can count seven trumps in your own hand plus two aces and two heart ruffs in dummy for a total of eleven tricks. To make a twelfth trick you will need to engineer a throw-in, forcing a defender to lead away from the king of spades. Where is the throw-in card? The fourth heart? No, that won't do. West will be short in spades and it is highly probable that East has the king. The only other possibility is a trump throw-in against East. That will involve giving up one of your winners and you will need to find compensation by scoring an established club trick in dummy.

Here is the complete deal.

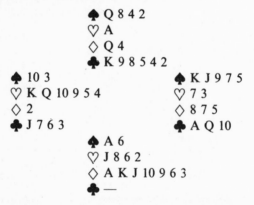

After ruffing the first club with the six of diamonds, you cross to the ace of hearts, ruff a club high, ruff a heart low, ruff another club high, and ruff another heart with the queen of diamonds. Yet another high club ruff puts you back in hand, and you continue with the ace, king and three of diamonds, throwing the lead to East who has to return a spade, allowing you to make two spades and a club at the end.

It was fortunate that West's singleton trump was the two. If East had held that card he might have countered the threat of the trump throw-in by unblocking his higher trumps under the ace and king, keeping his two to play under your three and leaving you in hand with two inescapable losers. He could also have found the unblocking defence if you had squandered the three of diamonds at trick one.

Try another defensive test.

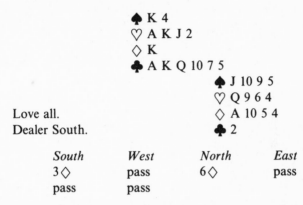

♠ K 4
♡ A K J 2
◇ K
♣ A K Q 10 7 5

　　　　　　　　　　　　♠ J 10 9 5
　　　　　　　　　　　　♡ Q 9 6 4
Love all.　　　　　　　◇ A 10 5 4
Dealer South.　　　　　♣ 2

South	West	North	East
3◇	pass	6◇	pass
pass	pass		

West leads the three of diamonds to dummy's king and your ace. How do you continue?

The switch to the jack of spades looks fairly automatic. Partner could produce the ace, after all, and if he doesn't you have given nothing away. Nothing except the contract, perhaps.

Automatic returns are for automatic players, not for those with card sense. It should be clear that you can always defeat this contract whether West has the ace of spades or not. All you have to do is safeguard your second trump trick.

Declarer presumably has seven diamonds, and there is danger only if he, like you, has a singleton club. In that case he might be able to reduce his trump length by ruffing three times and subsequently return to dummy to coup your trumps. To achieve this ending declarer needs four entries in dummy, and you can see that he has them—one club, one spade and two hearts. To thwart the hypothetical trump coup you must launch an immediate attack on the timing. A club return will do nothing to hinder declarer's trump reduction. Nor will a spade return if declarer can win in hand with the ace. The only entries in dummy that you can take out prematurely are those in hearts, and it is a heart switch that is required at trick two.

The complete deal:

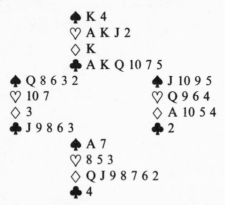

♠ K 4
♡ A K J 2
◇ K
♣ A K Q 10 7 5

♠ Q 8 6 3 2
♡ 10 7
◇ 3
♣ J 9 8 6 3

♠ J 10 9 5
♡ Q 9 6 4
◇ A 10 5 4
♣ 2

♠ A 7
♡ 8 5 3
◇ Q J 9 8 7 6 2
♣ 4

Your heart return actually creates a fifth entry in dummy, but declarer is unable to make use of it because you can discard hearts on the second and third rounds of clubs. Declarer may complete his trump reduction but he has no way of returning to dummy for the final trump coup, and eventually your ten of diamonds comes into its own.

Do you see what happens on the 'automatic' spade return? Declarer wins with the ace, tests the trumps with the queen of diamonds, then plays a club to the ace and ruffs a club. A heart to the king is followed by another club ruff, and declarer next makes use of the entry to dummy in the suit which you have been discarding on the clubs. He discards his losing heart on a top club and ruffs yet another club, reducing to two trumps. The remaining entry card then permits him to cross to the table and pick up your trumps with a plain suit lead.

Chapter 2

TABLE PRESENCE

The second attribute possessed in good measure by every master player is what is commonly known as 'table presence'. Again this is not an easy term to define, for table presence is a compound quality with several distinct ingredients. To a large degree it is based on an extension of the player's personality. We are each of us surrounded by our own invisible aura when we sit down at the bridge table, and this exerts an influence—hard to estimate but undeniable—on the behaviour of those with whom we play. The top player tends to put this extension of his personality to work for him, whether he means to or not.

When bridge was young, many champions achieved their results, in part at least, by browbeating tactics. The rudeness of certain experts was proverbial in those days, and this usually had the desired effect of reducing the opponents to such a state of nervousness or irritation that they failed to give of their best, thereby presenting the masters with undeserved successes. Such tactics were ethically wrong and today's experts are more circumspect. But each remains surrounded by a strong force-field, the purpose of which is to underline his own superiority. The approach varies, the style in each case reflecting the personality of the man. Some rely on a scornful glance and a curl of the lip to reduce an opponent to gibbering incompetence. Others glower and fume as if unable to believe that anyone could have the temerity to sit down and oppose them. There are the genial, talkative ones, who ostensibly treat their opponents as equals but still manage to induce in them the uneasy feeling that they are being toyed with by terrible jaws. And there are the quiet, unassuming ones who exude such an air of calm confidence as to give the impression of omnipotence.

There is no gainsaying the fact that big-name players enjoy an advantage in any bridge game which has nothing to do with their edge in skill. Many lesser players simply fail to play their normal game against them. Feeling the master's eye upon him, a player will often take some crazy action out of sheer nervousness. It's a sort of rabbit-and-stoat complex.

Another vital component of table presence is a heightened awareness, a hyper-sensitivity on the part of the expert to everything that is going on at the table. If you ask an expert what he would bid or play in a certain situation he will often decline to give you an answer, saying that he would need to be at the table to make a decision. He is not just being awkward; it is literally the truth. The expert relies to a large extent on 'table feel' to guide him in borderline situations. He needs to know the answers to certain questions before he will commit himself. Did East bid two spades reluctantly or confidently? In what tone of voice did West double four clubs? For how long did East pause on the fourth round? Did the opening lead hit the table at once or was it made after some thought?

When defending against an expert declarer it is advisable to keep a poker face at all times. He is quite likely to draw the correct inference from the fact that partner is still alert while you appear to have fallen asleep. The gleam in a defender's eye may tell him which way to finesse for a missing queen. A slight hesitation in choosing a discard may guide him to the winning line of play, even though it be against the odds. A charged atmosphere is meat and drink to the expert, who is often able to smell out a bad break simply by sensing the air of optimism emanating from some quarter. Nor is it safe for a defender to show the least reaction in the bidding. A quiver before passing may be all the expert needs to tell him that the trumps are stacked.

Here is an elementary test of your table presence. The setting is a team game against moderate opponents.

```
              ♠ J 9 8 3
              ♡ Q 4
              ◇ Q 8 4
              ♣ 9 8 7 3

              ♠ A K 7 6
              ♡ A 7 5
Game all.     ◇ 7 6 3
Dealer South. ♣ A K Q
```

South	West	North	East
2NT	pass	3♣	pass
3♠	pass	4♠	pass
pass	pass		

West leads the nine of hearts and when dummy goes down you see that you have reached a terrible contract. It looks like three diamonds and a heart to lose quite apart from any losers you may have in trumps.

Without much hope you try the queen of hearts from dummy. As expected East produces the king and you let him hold the trick. East cashes the ace and king of diamonds, West following with the five and the nine, and then plays the ten of clubs to your ace. How do you proceed?

Suddenly the prospects are a lot brighter. Your third diamond loser has disappeared and you have only to bring in the trumps without loss to make the game. There are two possible ways of playing the trumps. You can start with the ace and king, hoping to find someone with a doubleton queen, or you can take two trump finesses against East, using the diamond queen and a heart ruff as entries to dummy.

The odds favour playing to drop the queen of spades. Besides, you might argue that since East has already shown up with the king-jack of hearts and the ace-king of diamonds it would be only equitable for West to have the queen of spades, in which case the only chance is that it is doubleton.

But you must take a zero for table presence if you elect to play for the drop. The expert does not give a fig for the probabilities of distribution in this case, for he knows it to be a virtual certainty that East has both the queen and the ten of spades. Just consider the line of defence adopted. In cashing the ace and king of diamonds East committed an error so elementary that it would surely not have been made by any player beyond the beginner stage, *unless he had high expectations of scoring a trump trick as well*. With nothing of interest in trumps East would certainly have switched to a club at trick two.

The complete deal:

♠ J 9 8 3
♥ Q 4
♦ Q 8 4
♣ 9 8 7 3

♠ 4   ♠ Q 10 5 2
♥ 9 8 6 2   ♥ K J 10 3
♦ J 9 5   ♦ A K 10 2
♣ J 6 5 4 2   ♣ 10

♠ A K 7 6
♥ A 7 5
♦ 7 6 3
♣ A K Q

The expert enters dummy with the queen of diamonds and plays the jack of spades to the queen and king. The ace of hearts is cashed and the third heart is ruffed with the nine of spades to guard against the possibility of a 4–1 trump break. The eight of spades wins the next trick when East refuses to cover, and a further finesse against the ten of spades enables the declarer to draw the last trump and make the 'impossible' game.

In seeking to protect his potential trump trick East lost not only a diamond trick but also the trump trick itself. If he had switched to his club or continued hearts at trick two, the contract would have gone two down.

Here is another straightforward example of table presence. This time the setting was a pairs tournament, and again the opponents were not the strongest in the field.

> ♠ K 5
> ♡ J 9 3
> ◇ K 7 4 2
> ♣ A 9 4 3

> ♠ A 10
> ♡ Q 10 4
> ◇ A J 9 5
> ♣ Q J 10 8

N–S game.
Dealer South.

South	West	North	East
1♣	pass	3♣	pass
3NT	pass	pass	pass

The four of spades was led to the jack and ace. South saw that his contract depended on bringing in one of the minor suits without loss and he began by running the queen of clubs. East produced the king and returned the eight of spades to knock out the second stopper, West following with the two. Seeking further information, South played three more rounds of clubs ending in dummy. West discarded the five of hearts readily enough on the third club but took some time before parting with the three of spades on the next club. East threw the eight of hearts on this trick and declarer was at the crossroads.

On the face of it the best chance was to take a second-round diamond finesse against East, but South had an overwhelming conviction that the finesse would fail. All his instincts told him that

West had the queen of diamonds. Accordingly he played a low diamond to his ace, East playing the six and West the three. Now there was a further knotty decision to take. Obviously there was no chance if West held Q 10 3 in diamonds. Was West more likely to have Q 3 alone or Q 8 3?

The only clue—a slender one—lay in East's play. Holding 10 8 6 in diamonds, East might have tried to lead declarer astray by playing the eight on the first round. South therefore continued with the jack of diamonds and ran it when West produced the eight. That was the winning line, for the complete deal turned out to be:

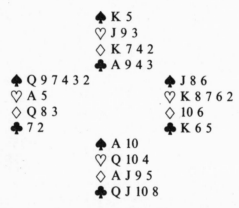

```
                    ♠ K 5
                    ♡ J 9 3
                    ◇ K 7 4 2
                    ♣ A 9 4 3
    ♠ Q 9 7 4 3 2              ♠ J 8 6
    ♡ A 5                      ♡ K 8 7 6 2
    ◇ Q 8 3                    ◇ 10 6
    ♣ 7 2                      ♣ K 6 5
                    ♠ A 10
                    ♡ Q 10 4
                    ◇ A J 9 5
                    ♣ Q J 10 8
```

When the score-sheet was examined it was seen that no other declarer had been successful in three notrumps. West was bitter about the result.

'It could only happen to me,' he complained. 'An expert ignores the odds and I get a bottom. How unlucky can you get.'

'I had a feeling that you had the queen of diamonds,' South said.

'How could you know that? You could know I had the queen of diamonds only if you had seen my hand.'

South forbore to reply, for it was clear that West did not comprehend the expert standard. He might have pointed out that he *had* seen West's hand—in his mind's eye. West had given him a glimpse of it by his hesitation on the fourth round of clubs.

Note that West might have misdirected declarer by dropping the eight of diamonds on the first round. South would then surely have played a low diamond next, hoping for the queen to fall. But a defender capable of such subtlety would not have hesitated on the fourth club.

A spectacular example of table presence comes from the *Sunday Times* Invitational Pairs contest of 1978. The French ace Henri Svarc found himself playing a dubious grand slam contract after some optimistic bidding.

♠ K Q 7 3
♡ —
♢ A K J 10 8 6
♣ A Q J

♠ 9 5   ♠ J 10 6
♡ A K Q 6 2   ♡ J 9 8 7 3
♢ 9 4 3   ♢ 7 5
♣ 7 6 5   ♣ K 10 2

♠ A 8 4 2
♡ 10 5 4
♢ Q 2
♣ 9 8 4 3

Game all.
Dealer East.

West	North	East	South
—	—	pass	pass
pass	1♢	pass	1♠
pass	3♣	pass	3♢
pass	3♠	pass	4♠
pass	5♡	pass	5♠
pass	6♡	pass	7♠
pass	pass	pass	

The opening lead of the ace of hearts was ruffed in dummy, East following with the three. The king and queen of spades won the next two tricks, and then Svarc paused to take stock. The straightforward line of play is to draw the last trump and then finesse twice in clubs, the ace of spades and the queen of diamonds providing the required entries to hand. As the cards lie this line of play is doomed, and Svarc diagnosed the position correctly from a couple of slender clues. West appeared to have a good heart holding since East had not encouraged on the opening lead, and yet West had passed originally. That made it seem somewhat unlikely that he would have the king of clubs. Furthermore, East appeared to be taking a keen interest in the defence.

Svarc had the courage to back his own judgment. He left the outstanding trump at large and tackled the diamonds. When the third diamond was played from the table East ruffed and South overruffed. He then crossed to the ace of clubs, discarded his losing clubs on the remaining diamonds, and led the queen of clubs for a ruffing finesse. East covered, declarer ruffed, and the last two tricks were made by dummy's trump and the jack of clubs.

East could not have done better by discarding on the diamonds instead of ruffing. Suppose East throws hearts in the hope of eventually overruffing dummy. After five rounds of diamonds the position is as follows:

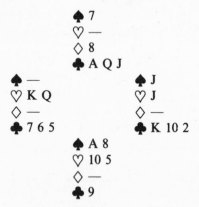

```
              ♠ 7
              ♡ —
              ♢ 8
              ♣ A Q J
  ♠ —                    ♠ J
  ♡ K Q                  ♡ J
  ♢ —                    ♢ —
  ♣ 7 6 5                ♣ K 10 2
              ♠ A 8
              ♡ 10 5
              ♢ —
              ♣ 9
```

It would be a mistake for declarer to play the sixth diamond at this point, for that would give East the chance to ditch his last heart. Svarc would undoubtedly have found the right play—the ace of clubs followed by the queen, finessing against East's king.

Subsequently a heart is ruffed in dummy, the last heart is discarded on the jack of clubs, and East's trump falls under the ace at trick thirteen.

Obviously this sixth sense that we call table presence is a thing worth cultivating if it can help to bring home contracts like that.

One final example: This hand, played by Maurizio Sementa of Italy in a match against a Monte Carlo team, won the 1978 'Hand of the Year' award of the International Bridge Press Association.

```
                    ♠ A 2
                    ♡ K Q J 4
                    ◇ A K Q 10 6 3
                    ♣ 3
      ♠ 3                        ♠ J 10 9 6 5
      ♡ 10 9 8 7                 ♡ 5
      ◇ 7 2                      ◇ J 9 8 5
      ♣ A K 9 8 5 2              ♣ Q 10 4
                    ♠ K Q 8 7 4
                    ♡ A 6 3 2
Game all.            ◇ 4
Dealer South.        ♣ J 7 6
```

South	*West*	*North*	*East*
1♠	pass	2◇	pass
2♡	pass	4NT	pass
5◇	pass	6♡	pass
pass	pass		

Yes, they open the bidding pretty light in Italy. West led the ace of clubs and continued with the king which was ruffed in dummy, East following with the four and the ten. Declarer cashed the king and queen of hearts, East discarding a spade on the second round. The 4–1 trump split was a bit of a blow, but the slam would still be safe enough if either the spades or the diamonds broke evenly. Accordingly, declarer continued with the jack of hearts on which East discarded another spade.

The spade discards seemed ominous. That was the suit South had opened, after all. Of course, it could be a piece of misdirection by East with the spades breaking 3–3 all the time. If the spade discards had been forced, however, it must mean that East began with a 5–1–4–3 pattern, in which case declarer would not be able to enter his hand on the second round of spades because West would ruff.

Sensing the spade discards to be genuine, Sementa took his only remaining chance. After the jack of hearts he played the two of spades to his queen, leaving this position:

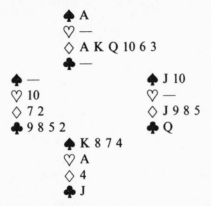

Sementa drew West's last trump with his ace and discarded the ace of spades from the table! Now East found himself in the grip of a progressive triple squeeze. Clearly a spade or a diamond discard would be fatal, so he chose to part with the queen of clubs, hoping that his partner had the jack. Declarer had that card, however, and he promptly cashed it to squeeze East again in spades and diamonds, thus landing a well-played slam.

It is worth noting that the slam can be defeated if West continues with a low club instead of the king at trick two. That is a difficult defence, but it might have been found if East had played the ten of clubs on the first round.

Chapter 3

THROUGH THE BACKS
OF THE CARDS

We move on to consider that aspect of the game which most people consider to be the hallmark of the expert—skill at card-reading. Every bridge player knows something about card-reading and practises it to a certain extent. In the master player, card-reading ability is developed to such a degree that it appears like black magic to the uninitiated. The expert plays many hands in double-dummy fashion, as though he had the uncanny gift of being able to see through the backs of the cards.

How is the effect achieved? Well, card-reading skill is really an amalgam of several skills, all of which can be developed by practice. The solid foundation on which everything rests is the ability to count the hand. Counting the unseen hands can be a laborious business when you first attempt it, but it soon ceases to be a chore and becomes a valuable aid to your technique. The location of the enemy honour cards can often be deduced with fair accuracy by reference to the bidding, or lack of bidding, on the part of the opponents. The opening lead provides an additional source of information. By a process of logical deduction the expert builds up a picture of the unseen hands which is often sufficiently accurate to enable him to plan the play on double-dummy lines. He will not always get the picture absolutely right, but he will do so often enough to justify his reputation for being able to see through the backs of the cards.

When unable to obtain a complete count of the hand, the expert will happily make do with a hypothetical count based on the bidding, the early play and the discards. Furthermore, if a card has to be located in a particular defender's hand to give the contract a chance of success, the expert will assume that it is so located and play on that assumption. When it comes off, his reputation for wizardry is enhanced.

Counting is of particular importance in defence. Here is a test of your defensive card-reading.

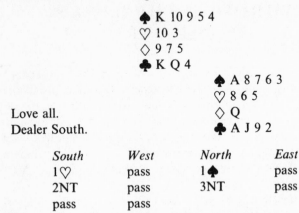

```
                    ♠ K 10 9 5 4
                    ♡ 10 3
                    ◇ 9 7 5
                    ♣ K Q 4
                                    ♠ A 8 7 6 3
                                    ♡ 8 6 5
Love all.                           ◇ Q
Dealer South.                       ♣ A J 9 2
```

South	West	North	East
South	*West*	*North*	*East*
1♡	pass	1♠	pass
2NT	pass	3NT	pass
pass	pass		

West leads the four of diamonds and South plays the six under your queen. You switch to the eight of hearts on which South plays the ace and West the four. The three of clubs is led to the seven, king and ace, and South wins the heart return with the king as West completes an echo with the two. Declarer crosses to the queen of clubs and plays a third club from dummy. You win with the jack as partner discards the two of diamonds. What do you do now?

A complete count of the hand is available. Partner led the four of diamonds and has discarded the two, which indicates that he started with a five-card suit. His echo in hearts tells of four cards in that suit, he followed twice in clubs, and he must therefore have two spades. Declarer's jump to two notrumps was a trifle unorthodox on his 1–4–4–4 pattern. South must surely have all the heart honours plus the two top diamonds to justify his bid.

Is the danger clear? You must cash the ace of spades before

exiting in hearts or clubs; otherwise partner may find himself in trouble when declarer runs his winners.

The complete deal:

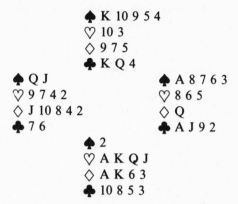

Suppose East fails to cash the ace of spades and returns his fourth club in this position:

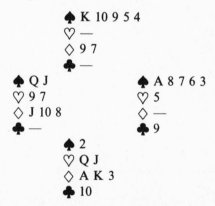

West can throw a heart on the fourth club, but he has no good discard when declarer cashes two more hearts. The jaws of the squeeze aptly named 'The Vice' by Terence Reese close around his queen and jack of spades. When West parts with one of his spade honours, South cashes the top diamonds and leads a spade, and East has to yield a spade trick to dummy at the end.

I defended this hand in the West seat partnered by Scottish International John MacLaren. At the critical point MacLaren cashed the ace of spades, leaving the declarer with no play for game.

Try another card-reading test.

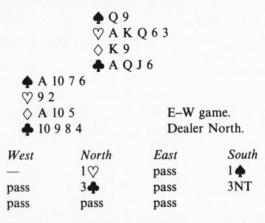

	♠ Q 9		
	♡ A K Q 6 3		
	◇ K 9		
	♣ A Q J 6		

♠ A 10 7 6			
♡ 9 2			
◇ A 10 5		E–W game.	
♣ 10 9 8 4		Dealer North.	

West	*North*	*East*	*South*
—	1♡	pass	1♠
pass	3♣	pass	3NT
pass	pass	pass	

Your lead of the ten of clubs is covered by the jack, and East wins the trick with the king. East switches to the jack of spades, which is allowed to run to dummy's queen. South plays out the ace, king and queen of hearts, discarding the three of diamonds on the third round. What is your discard?

Clearly you are not going to discard a club. The choice lies between spades and diamonds. Declarer bid spades and it seems natural to discard a diamond, keeping your spade length intact. But let's look a little more deeply into the position.

For his bidding declarer must surely have the queen and jack of diamonds as well as the king of spades. At that, he has only six points. Declarer's next move will be to play the king of diamonds from dummy (he will not be so foolish as to play a fourth heart), and you will know the diamond count as soon as the suit is played. You will have to hold up your ace until the second round, and you can get off lead easily enough with a club. But suppose declarer then plays two more rounds of clubs, throwing the lead to you once again. Yes, that's the danger. You must take care not to be left with nothing but spades in your hand at that point, for you would have to yield the contract by giving South a spade and a further diamond trick.

The third diamond must therefore be retained as an exit card. You should discard a spade on the third heart.

The complete deal:

```
              ♠ Q 9
              ♡ A K Q 6 3
              ◇ K 9
              ♣ A Q J 6
  ♠ A 10 7 6              ♠ J 3 2
  ♡ 9 2                   ♡ J 8·5 4
  ◇ A 10 5                ◇ 8 6 2
  ♣ 10 9 8 4              ♣ K 7 2
              ♠ K 8 5 4
              ♡ 10 7
              ◇ Q J 7 4 3
              ♣ 5 3
```

Be sure to congratulate partner on that return of the jack of spades, without which there would have been no defeating this contract. Once you have discarded a spade on the third heart you have an answer to anything declarer may try. If he keeps two spades in his hand after the clubs have gone, you simply exit with the third diamond and South has to give you two spade tricks at the end.

The initial lead of a low spade would have made your task somewhat easier as it happens.

It is not only in defence that card-reading has a major role to play. Here is a problem in declarer play:

```
                    ♠ K 8 6 3
                    ♡ 8 3
                    ◇ A K 9 5 4 2
                    ♣ 10

                    ♠ 5 2
                    ♡ A Q J 10 5 4
Game all.           ◇ —
Dealer East.        ♣ Q 8 7 6 3
```

West	North	East	South
—	—	1♠	2♠*
dble	pass	pass	3♣
pass	3◇	pass	3♡
dble	pass	pass	pass

*Michaels cue bid, showing hearts and another suit.

West leads the ace of spades against your contract of three hearts doubled. After a look at dummy he switches to the two of hearts. You try the eight from the table, but East produces the nine and you win the trick with the jack. How should you continue?

You appear to have five trump tricks in your own hand. The king of spades, if it stands up, will give you a sixth trick, and the top diamonds will bring your tally up to eight. In order to score a ninth trick you will need to ruff a club in dummy.

On the bidding it seems probable that the trumps will be divided 4–1, and you must try to avoid losing a club to West since a further trump lead would ruin your plan. West is marked with the ace of spades and the king of hearts, and it is reasonable to place both top club honours with East to account for his opening bid. You might therefore consider crossing to dummy with the king of spades, taking your discards on the diamonds, and then leading the club from the table.

Unfortunately this plan contains the seeds of its own failure. When East comes in with a top club he will shoot back a spade, promoting a second trump trick for his partner, who holds K 7 6 of trumps over your A Q 10.

The clubs have to be tackled in a more direct way. The correct move is to play the queen of clubs from hand at trick three.

The complete deal:

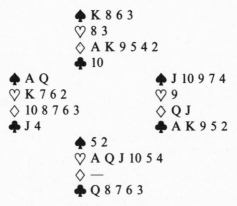

East has to win the club trick and there is nothing he can do to defeat the contract. You win a spade return in dummy, cash the top diamonds, ruff a diamond in hand, ruff a club on the table, ruff another diamond in hand, and claim two further tricks with your A Q 10 of trumps.

West lost his chance of defeating the contract when he led his ace 'to have a look at dummy'. If he had led a trump originally and continued with a second trump when in with the ace of spades, you would have been held to eight tricks.

```
                              ♠ 6
                              ♡ K 8 3
                              ◇ A J 8 4 3
                              ♣ K Q 9 5
                                              ♠ J 9 7 4 3
                                              ♡ A Q 10 6
Game all.                                     ◇ K 9 5
Dealer South.                                 ♣ 3

            South      West       North      East
            1♣         pass       1◇         pass
            1♠         pass       2♡         pass
            3♣         pass       5♣         pass
            pass       pass
```

West leads the seven of clubs, dummy plays the five and South wins with the eight. Declarer plays a diamond to the ace, ruffs a diamond with the two of clubs, cashes the ace and king of spades, discarding a heart from the table, and then leads the five of hearts on which West plays the two and dummy the king. What do you play after winning the ace of hearts?

Declarer's hand pattern is clear from the bidding and the play. He began with five clubs, four spades, three hearts and a diamond. South has already scored five tricks and if he manages to make his remaining trumps separately he will be home. Clearly a diamond return is out, for that would supply the extra entry South needs to ruff all dummy's diamonds in his hand.

What about a spade return? That appears to upset declarer's timing for the crossruff, for he will be able to ruff only two spades in dummy and two diamonds in hand before giving up the lead again in hearts. However, if you look more closely into the position you will see that a spade return is not good enough. South will ruff in dummy, ruff a diamond in hand and lead his fourth spade. If West discards on this trick, South will throw the last heart from dummy, putting you on lead again and clearing his communications for a complete crossruff. If West ruffs the fourth spade, of course, South can overruff in dummy and establish a second diamond trick.

That leaves only the heart suit, and naturally you must not cash the queen for that again would clear the way for a complete crossruff. You need to pass the lead to partner who has a trump to return. After winning the ace of hearts, therefore, you must continue with the six of hearts in the hope that partner has the jack.

The complete deal:

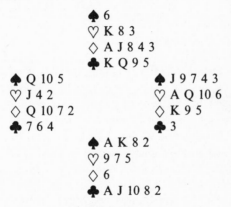

When partner produces the jack of hearts and shoots back a trump, declarer has no chance of making more than ten tricks.

An initial lead of the jack of hearts would have defeated the contract rather more easily, of course. Indeed, on the bidding quite a good case can be made for this lead. When South reverted to clubs over his partner's fourth-suit bid of two hearts he denied possession of any sort of heart stopper.

♠ Q J 6 5 3
♡ A K Q 6
◇ 8 2
♣ K 5

♠ A 4
♡ 10 8 7 3
◇ A J 10 4
♣ A Q 7

Game all.
Dealer South.

South	West	North	East
1NT	pass	2♣	pass
2♡	pass	4NT	pass
5♠	pass	6♡	pass
pass	pass		

West leads the jack of clubs to dummy's king, and you see that in spite of partner's crude bidding you have landed in a reasonable contract. When you test the hearts with the ace and king and West discards a club on the second round, however, it doesn't look so good.

Now you can't afford a spade loser. When you lead the queen of spades East covers with the king and your ace wins. How should you continue?

It's a matter of accurate timing now. There will be no problem if the spades divide 3–3, but if East has only two spades you will have to play your cards in precisely the right order. It would be a mistake to play a second spade at this point, because you cannot afford to play a third round of spades until you have taken your diamond discard in dummy on the third round of clubs. So the first move must be to cash the ace and queen of clubs, discarding a diamond from the table.

Now it would be premature to cash the diamond ace and ruff a diamond. Spade establishment must be one of your threats, and the right move at this point is a spade to dummy's jack and a third round of spades for a ruff. If the suit breaks 3–3 you can just play a trump to dummy's queen and continue spades, losing only a trump trick. In fact the complete deal turns out to be:

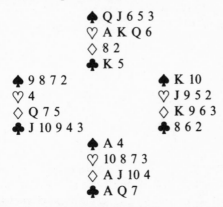

♠ Q J 6 5 3
♡ A K Q 6
◇ 8 2
♣ K 5

♠ 9 8 7 2   ♠ K 10
♡ 4   ♡ J 9 5 2
◇ Q 7 5   ◇ K 9 6 3
♣ J 10 9 4 3   ♣ 8 6 2

♠ A 4
♡ 10 8 7 3
◇ A J 10 4
♣ A Q 7

On the third round of spades East has no good move to make. If he ruffs high and returns a trump, you win in dummy and establish the spades with a ruff. If East discards on the third spade, you ruff in hand, cash the ace of diamonds, ruff a diamond with the six of trumps and lead another spade. Again, if East ruffs high and returns a trump the spade suit is established. And if he discards you make your trumps separately to chalk up twelve tricks.

Do you see why it would have been a mistake to play a second round of spades before cashing the clubs? After discarding a diamond from dummy on the third club, you would have had to enter dummy by means of a second-round diamond ruff. Then the timing would have been wrong. When you led a spade from dummy East would ruff high and return his remaining trump, giving you no further chance. With the spades not yet established, you would be left with an inescapable diamond loser in hand.

```
              ♠ 9 6 3 2
              ♡ 5 4
              ◇ K J 7 6
              ♣ 10 8 2
  ♠ A K J 7 5
  ♡ K Q 9 3
  ◇ 8 4 2                          Love all.
  ♣ K                              Dealer West.
```

West	North	East	South
1♠	pass	1NT	2♡
dble	pass	pass	3♣
pass	pass	dble	pass
pass	pass		

You start with the ace and king of spades, East following with the eight and the queen, South with the four and the ten. On your switch to the eight of diamonds dummy plays the six, East the queen and declarer the ten. Partner returns the three of clubs and, after a little thought, declarer goes up with the ace, felling your king. South next cashes the ace of hearts and continues with the jack of hearts to your queen, East playing the two and then the ten of hearts. How should you continue?

Declarer's hand pattern appears to be 2–5–1–5, while partner has a 2–2–5–4 shape. A lot will depend on the quality of partner's trumps. He is unlikely to have an honour, but if he can overruff dummy's eight you will probably have nothing to worry about. The danger is that partner's trumps may all be midgets, in which case declarer will score five trumps in his own hand plus two ruffs in dummy. The ace of hearts is his eighth trick, and if he can make a diamond trick by ruffing out partner's ace he will be home.

How can you prevent declarer from scoring that diamond trick? There is only one way and that is to switch back to spades, playing the jack to let partner start shedding his diamonds. The fact that you establish the nine of spades as a winner on the table is neither here nor there, for declarer will not be able to enjoy that card because of partner's trumps.

The complete deal:

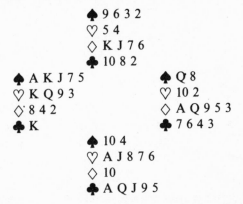

```
                  ♠ 9 6 3 2
                  ♡ 5 4
                  ◇ K J 7 6
                  ♣ 10 8 2
  ♠ A K J 7 5                    ♠ Q 8
  ♡ K Q 9 3                      ♡ 10 2
  ◇ 8 4 2                        ◇ A Q 9 5 3
  ♣ K                            ♣ 7 6 4 3
                  ♠ 10 4
                  ♡ A J 8 7 6
                  ◇ 10
                  ♣ A Q J 9 5
```

East discards a diamond on the jack of spades and South ruffs. Next comes a heart ruff with the eight of clubs, East discarding another diamond. Scorning the nine of spades, South plays the king of diamonds and ruffs out East's ace. When another heart is ruffed in dummy, however, East's last diamond goes away and declarer is left with two established winners in dummy which he cannot use. Eventually East scores the setting trick with one of his trumps.

Declarer did some useful card-reading himself on this hand. Once East had shown up with the ace and queen of diamonds and the queen of spades, South realized that he could not have the king of clubs. He took his only chance by going up with the ace and was rewarded by the fall of your king. Also worth noting is the play of the jack of hearts on the second round, designed to prevent a killing trump return by keeping East off lead. South really deserved to make his contract, and he *would* have made it against many defenders.

You defeat the contract rather more easily if you switch to the king of clubs at trick three, but that is double-dummy defence.

```
                        ♠ 7 5 3
                        ♡ J 6 2
                        ◇ Q 9 4
                        ♣ K 10 9 4


                        ♠ A J 10 9 8
                        ♡ A K 10 7 4
        N–S game.       ◇ 6
        Dealer South.   ♣ A Q
```

South	West	North	East
1♠	dble	1NT	2◇
3♡	pass	3♠	pass
4♠	pass	pass	pass

West leads the ace of diamonds and, on receiving an encouraging seven from East, continues with the three of diamonds to the nine and jack. You ruff and cash the ace of spades, dropping the queen from West. A second trump goes to West's king, and West continues with the ten of diamonds to the queen, king and ruff. How should you continue?

You have only one trump left in each hand and you can hardly afford to draw East's last trump at this point, for the defenders would score at least one more diamond trick when they gained the lead.

What do you know about the distribution? West appears to have started with four diamonds and two spades, leaving him seven cards in the other two suits. If the hearts are 3–2 you can make the contract readily enough by playing ace, king and another heart. However, West has little enough in the way of high-card strength for his double and it seems likely that he will have four hearts. How do you cope with a 4–1 heart split?

One line of play that may occur to you is to cash one top heart, then overtake the queen of clubs with dummy's king and play a second heart from the table. If East uses his trump 'on air' you will be able to establish the hearts without difficulty. If East discards, you can win and play a third heart, and again you will have no trouble in establishing the heart suit. Or will you? Yes, there is a snag. East will discard a club on the second heart and another club on the third heart. On winning the heart queen West will continue with a fourth heart which you will have to ruff in dummy. East will discard his fourth and last club on this trick, and you will have no way of returning to hand to draw his trump.

You can succeed against a 4–1 heart split only if West has the jack of clubs as well. The correct line is to cash the ace of clubs, overtake the queen of clubs with dummy's king and continue with the ten of clubs to throw West in. The complete deal:

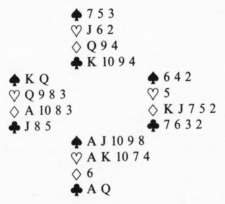

```
              ♠ 7 5 3
              ♡ J 6 2
              ◇ Q 9 4
              ♣ K 10 9 4
♠ K Q                          ♠ 6 4 2
♡ Q 9 8 3                      ♡ 5
◇ A 10 8 3                     ◇ K J 7 5 2
♣ J 8 5                        ♣ 7 6 3 2
              ♠ A J 10 9 8
              ♡ A K 10 7 4
              ◇ 6
              ♣ A Q
```

You discard a heart on the third club and West, in with the jack, has to lead a heart or concede a ruff and discard, solving your problem in either case. West may, of course, try to evade the throw-in by playing his jack of clubs on the first or second round. Then you simply cash your four club tricks and draw the last trump, conceding a heart to the queen at the end.

Of course you may finish with egg on your face if the hearts are 3–2 all the time. The expert relies on his nose in situations like this and is not afraid of looking silly once in a while.

Here is a tough defensive problem.

```
                    ♠ A J 10 9
                    ♡ A K 6 3
                    ◇ 6
                    ♣ Q J 6 5
                                    ♠ 8 7 6 4 2
                                    ♡ 10 8 2
        N–S game.                   ◇ A 5
        Dealer West.                ♣ 7 3 2
```

West	North	East	South
1◇	dble	pass	1NT
pass	2◇	pass	2♠
pass	3♠	pass	4♠
pass	pass	pass	

West leads the king of diamonds. How do you plan the defence?

For a start, how many trumps do you think South has? Surely he must have three only, for with four he would have bid spades rather than notrumps on the first round of bidding. So partner will have a trump, and it is perhaps a pity that he did not lead it. Still, if it seems a good idea you can always win the first trick with the ace of diamonds and switch to trumps yourself.

The trouble with that line of defence is that you will never get in again to play a second round of trumps. Declarer is likely to have one of the high club honours (the contract will be easily defeated if partner has both), and if he can score four trumps in dummy plus two ruffs in hand, two heart and two club tricks will give him his game.

Since you cannot profitably attack declarer's trumps, is there any way of attacking his side winners? Yes, it may be possible to deny him a second club trick if you can manage to discard one of your club losers before he can get the suit going. Clearly you must overtake the king of diamonds and continue the suit, hoping to force dummy to ruff. When partner gains the lead with his club honour another high diamond will force dummy to ruff again as one of your clubs goes away.

The complete deal:

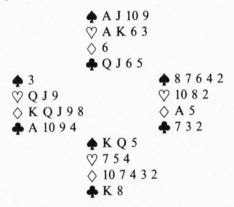

```
                    ♠ A J 10 9
                    ♡ A K 6 3
                    ◇ 6
                    ♣ Q J 6 5
        ♠ 3                        ♠ 8 7 6 4 2
        ♡ Q J 9                    ♡ 10 8 2
        ◇ K Q J 9 8                ◇ A 5
        ♣ A 10 9 4                 ♣ 7 3 2
                    ♠ K Q 5
                    ♡ 7 5 4
                    ◇ 10 7 4 3 2
                    ♣ K 8
```

Once you have prevented South from enjoying two club tricks, the weight of your 8 7 6 of trumps is enough to stop declarer's five of trumps scoring a trick. You need some co-operation from partner, however. Suppose declarer ruffs the second diamond in dummy and plays the queen of clubs. Partner must hold up his ace in order to deny declarer an extra entry to hand.

Do you see what would happen if West won the ace of clubs immediately? The diamond return would be ruffed in dummy and a club to the king would be followed by a third diamond ruff. After cashing the ace and king of hearts, declarer would lead a club from dummy in this position:

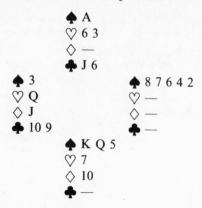

```
              ♠ A
              ♡ 6 3
              ◇ —
              ♣ J 6
  ♠ 3                    ♠ 8 7 6 4 2
  ♡ Q                    ♡ —
  ◇ J                    ◇ —
  ♣ 10 9                 ♣ —
              ♠ K Q 5
              ♡ 7
              ◇ 10
              ♣ —
```

South would overruff your spade six with his queen, ruff his last diamond with the ace of spades, and play the last club. When you ruffed with the seven of spades he would discard his losing heart, retaining K 5 of spades over your 8 4 and making the last two tricks.

It is quite a difficult defence and your task would certainly have been simpler if partner had led his trump originally. If you missed your way on this one, you can console yourself with the reflection that you are in good company. The winning defence was not found when the hand turned up in an international match between England and Wales.

Chapter 4

THE INNER GAME

In the field of physical sports a great deal of attention is paid nowadays to the concept of 'the inner game'. Teachers and coaches are beginning to recognize that the most important battle is the one that goes on in a player's mind. Basically this is a battle to achieve tranquillity, and it is a battle that each individual must win for himself before he can hope to produce his best form.

Take tennis as an example. Many problems can be traced to trying too hard. Anxiety generates tension, which results in the faults of 'pressing' or 'snatching'. The body of a top-class tennis player is familiar with all the actions that are required of it and is quite capable of performing them without conscious direction from the mind. A sudden, sharp message from the brain can, in fact, be counter-productive, upsetting the fine balance of the player's game and resulting in a mishit shot.

Those who study the inner game try to cultivate a state of mind that is watchful yet relaxed, where decisions are taken subconsciously as far as is possible. With the body free to get on with the job that it does so well, the player's game develops a rhythmic flow and his timing improves miraculously. Soon he is in a state of total absorption, knowing a sense of oneness with his racket, with the ball, with the court and even with his opponent. Some have gone as far as to describe this as a profound spiritual experience.

It is much the same with bridge. Although no physical element is involved, most of the mental activity should take place at the subconscious level. Concentration is always necessary, of course, but it should be a relaxed concentration. The aim should be to take as few conscious decisions as possible.

49

That is how the experts manage to stay fresh throughout the course of a long championship. They may bid and play sixty hands a day for a fortnight, but the mental energy they expend is not excessive since most of the work is done in their subconscious minds. Experience and technique carry them through all the routine situations, leaving them with energy to spare for anything unusual that needs to be analysed comprehensively. Even then the expert does not normally make an all-out assault on the problem, but examines it calmly from all angles before committing himself to a line of play. He knows that an excess of zeal can be fatal to his peace of mind.

This is not to say that the expert plays in top form all the time. Naturally there will be days when his mental attitude is not fully under control. But every expert knows the deep satisfaction of those occasions when he puts it all together, when he sees the cards well and reads their message clearly, when his mind meshes harmoniously with that of his partner and his game slips into a groove in which the right decisions seem to be made without conscious effort. On such a day it appears to be wellnigh impossible to make a mistake.

No one can hope to achieve this ideal state of mind every time he sits down to play. Relaxed concentration is the goal, and it can be reached only when the battle for inner tranquillity has been won. It takes a calm and unflustered mind to apply the calipers of judgment to each situation as it arises at the bridge table.

Try a new approach on the problems that follow. Relax and let your subconscious mind do the thinking. You may be surprised by how much it knows about the game.

First a defensive test:

```
          ♠ J 10 6 4 2
          ♡ 9
          ◇ J 10 4 2
          ♣ A J 5
♠ 7 5 3
♡ Q 10 7 6
◇ A K 6 3                    Love all.
♣ 10 2                       Dealer West.
```

West	North	East	South
pass	pass	pass	1NT*
pass	2♡†	pass	2♠
pass	pass	pass	

*12–14   † transfer to spades

You lead the ace of diamonds on which East plays the seven and South the eight. How should you continue?

The five of diamonds is missing and it looks as though partner has started an echo. Presumably he will be able to ruff the third round of the suit. But can it be right to give him his ruff straight away? Certainly not, your subconscious mind replies, for in giving partner the diamond ruff you would also be setting up a diamond trick for declarer.

Besides, apart from your two diamond tricks and partner's ruff, you need three further tricks if the contract is to be defeated. Partner will need to have at least one trump trick. He may have a trump trick, the ace of hearts, and a club trick, for instance, or even two trump tricks and the ace of hearts. A third possibility is that partner may be able to give you a third-round club ruff.

Whatever the position it must be a good move to attack clubs at trick two. Partner may not be able to tackle the suit from his side of the table. Every real bridge player will feel an overwhelming urge to lead the ten of clubs. Don't fight it. Let your subconscious mind have its way.

The complete deal:

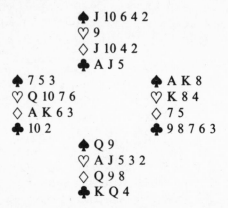

```
            ♠ J 10 6 4 2
            ♡ 9
            ◇ J 10 4 2
            ♣ A J 5
♠ 7 5 3                      ♠ A K 8
♡ Q 10 7 6                   ♡ K 8 4
◇ A K 6 3                    ◇ 7 5
♣ 10 2                       ♣ 9 8 7 6 3
            ♠ Q 9
            ♡ A J 5 3 2
            ◇ Q 9 8
            ♣ K Q 4
```

When East wins the first round of trumps he will play a second club, and you will eventually score a ruff in both minor suits to put the contract one down. South may, of course, try the effect of playing a second diamond at trick three, but you can counter, after winning your king, by leading a second club yourself. Once partner shows up with nothing in clubs you know he must have something in trumps, so the diamond ruff can wait.

Would it be the same if you continued diamonds at tricks two and three? After scoring his ruff partner could switch to a club himself. Well, you might get away with it, but declarer would have a chance to take advantage of your faulty timing. After winning the first club South could play a spade to knock out East's king. The second club would be won in dummy and the jack of diamonds led for a club discard. If East ruffed, that would be the end of the defence. And if East discarded, South could himself ruff dummy's third club with his remaining trump. After the ace of hearts and a heart ruff, a trump from the table would again restrict the defence to five tricks.

It takes a club switch by West at trick two to make sure of defeating the contract.

Now try a problem in declarer play.

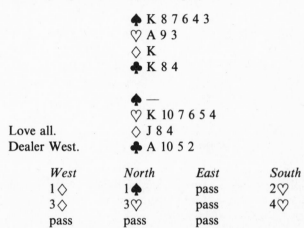

♠ K 8 7 6 4 3
♡ A 9 3
♢ K
♣ K 8 4

♠ —
♡ K 10 7 6 5 4
♢ J 8 4
♣ A 10 5 2

Love all.
Dealer West.

West	North	East	South
1♢	1♠	pass	2♡
3♢	3♡	pass	4♡
pass	pass	pass	

West leads the nine of clubs to the four, jack and ace. You concede a diamond to West's ace, East playing the two, and West continues with the seven of clubs to dummy's king. When you ruff a small spade in hand, East plays the ten and West the two. How should you continue?

You are in a position to ruff your remaining diamonds in dummy, and it looks as though your only losers should be a diamond, a club and a trump. However, you must time the play carefully in order to allow for the possibility of a 4–0 trump break. After all, it is more than a little suspicious that West did not switch to a trump when he was in with the ace of diamonds.

Those who bring a calm and relaxed concentration to bear on the problem will see that nothing can be lost by conceding a club to East's queen at this point. That is the only correct play.

The complete deal:

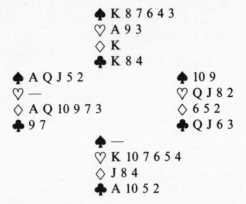

Suppose East returns a diamond (as good as anything). You ruff on the table, ruff another spade and play the ten of clubs, which wins a trick. You ruff the last diamond, cash the ace of hearts, and lead another spade in this position:

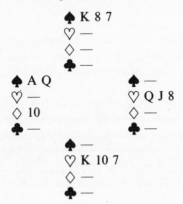

When East ruffs high you underruff with the seven and claim the last two tricks.

The timing is wrong for the coup if the clubs are not cleared before you ruff the third diamond in dummy. Try it for yourself and see.

Here is a deal that affords an opportunity for fine play by both sides.

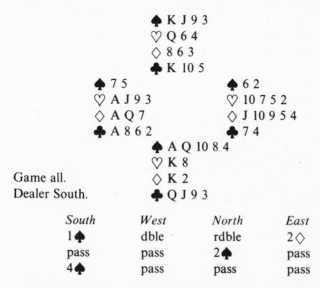

```
                    ♠ K J 9 3
                    ♡ Q 6 4
                    ◇ 8 6 3
                    ♣ K 10 5
      ♠ 7 5                         ♠ 6 2
      ♡ A J 9 3                     ♡ 10 7 5 2
      ◇ A Q 7                       ◇ J 10 9 5 4
      ♣ A 8 6 2                     ♣ 7 4
                    ♠ A Q 10 8 4
                    ♡ K 8
Game all.           ◇ K 2
Dealer South.       ♣ Q J 9 3
```

South	West	North	East
1♠	dble	rdble	2◇
pass	pass	2♠	pass
4♠	pass	pass	pass

Holding the aces in all three side suits, West chooses the passive lead of a trump. South draws a second round of trumps and takes a moment to consider his prospects. There are four potential losers—a heart, two diamonds and a club—and it is clear that some sort of end play will be required to produce the tenth trick.

Naturally the club suit has to be tackled first. South plays a club to dummy's king and returns a club to his queen. West may well take his ace at this point and return the suit, fearing to be thrown in later to lead one of the red suits or concede a ruff and discard.

On winning the third round of clubs, South leads the eight of hearts from hand. West has to play low to avoid giving declarer two heart tricks and dummy's queen wins the trick. Now South returns to hand with a trump and cashes the fourth club, discarding a heart from dummy. Finally he leads the king of hearts in this position to throw West on lead:

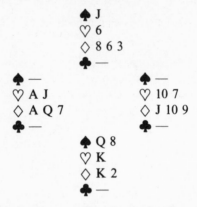

```
              ♠ J
              ♡ 6
              ◇ 8 6 3
              ♣ —

♠ —                        ♠ —
♡ A J                      ♡ 10 7
◇ A Q 7                    ◇ J 10 9
♣ —                        ♣ —

              ♠ Q 8
              ♡ K
              ◇ K 2
              ♣ —
```

Winning the ace of hearts, West is caught after all in the throw-in that he feared. He must either concede a ruff and discard by playing another heart or allow declarer to score his king of diamonds.

However, an expert in the West seat enjoying that relaxed state of watchfulness that constitutes good form, would not have been caught in this trap. Noting his partner's echo in clubs, he would have realized that he could afford to hold up the ace of clubs once more. He would have taken his ace on the third round and returned his fourth club, and the timing for South's 'Dilemma Coup' would have been ruined.

The essential difference is that South is forced to find a discard from dummy on the fourth round of clubs *before* he has had the opportunity of slipping past the ace of hearts. If he discards a heart, West can play the ace of hearts on the first round and return the suit. If declarer elects to discard a diamond from dummy, he is subsequently unable to eliminate the heart suit. Whatever he does, the contract has to go one down.

When both declarer and the defenders are seeing the ball well and taking it sweetly in the middle of the racket, the possibilities of move and countermove can be fascinating.

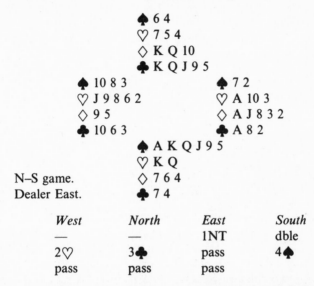

```
                    ♠ 6 4
                    ♡ 7 5 4
                    ◇ K Q 10
                    ♣ K Q J 9 5
     ♠ 10 8 3                    ♠ 7 2
     ♡ J 9 8 6 2                 ♡ A 10 3
     ◇ 9 5                       ◇ A J 8 3 2
     ♣ 10 6 3                    ♣ A 8 2
                    ♠ A K Q J 9 5
                    ♡ K Q
N–S game.           ◇ 7 6 4
Dealer East.        ♣ 7 4
```

West	North	East	South
—	—	1NT	dble
2♡	3♣	pass	4♠
pass	pass	pass	

West leads the nine of diamonds and the king is played from dummy. East has an immediate decision to make. Judging correctly that his partner is more likely to have a doubleton than a singleton, he allows dummy's king to win the first trick. This has the effect of denying declarer a later entry in diamonds once the clubs have been established.

South draws trumps in three rounds, West echoing to give his partner the count. The queen of hearts is now played to East's ace. West plays the two on this trick, and East is faced with another crucial decision. Suppose he makes the natural return of a heart. South wins with the king and leads a club to dummy's jack. East must hold up his ace to shut out the club suit, and South makes good use of this entry to dummy by ruffing a heart, thereby removing East's last exit card. When South continues with a club to dummy's queen, East is helpless.

This is the position:

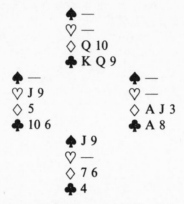

```
              ♠ —
              ♡ —
              ◇ Q 10
              ♣ K Q 9
  ♠ —                      ♠ —
  ♡ J 9                    ♡ —
  ◇ 5                      ◇ A J 3
  ♣ 10 6                   ♣ A 8
              ♠ J 9
              ♡ —
              ◇ 7 6
              ♣ 4
```

The best East can do, after winning the ace of clubs, is to cash the ace of diamonds and hold South to ten tricks.

However, an expert defender at the top of his form would not have given declarer the chance to play so well. A sufficient count of the hand was available. West was known from his echo to have started with three trumps, and his two of hearts indicated an odd number of cards—obviously five—in the suit. From the start East had assumed his partner to have two diamonds, which left him with three clubs. It followed that declarer had precisely two clubs, and East would have seen that, after winning the ace of hearts, he could make sure of killing dummy's club suit by switching to a low club.

What a difference this makes to the timing of the play! South is reluctantly forced to win his club trick before he has had a chance to unblock the hearts. As a result he cannot eliminate the hearts from East's hand. When East eventually comes in with the ace of clubs he can exit safely with his third heart and wait for his two diamond tricks.

It is worth noting that declarer has no problems on any lead other than a diamond.

The next hand is an exercise in pure timing. To start with we shall look at only two hands.

```
        ♠ 7 5 4 2
        ♡ Q J 6
        ◇ 9 3
        ♣ 6 5 4 3

        ♠ Q J 9 8 3
        ♡ 10 8
        ◇ A K Q J 10 4
        ♣ —
```

Love all.
Dealer West.

West	North	East	South
1♣	pass	1NT	2◇
4♡	pass	pass	4♠
5♣	5♠	dble	pass
pass	pass		

West leads the ace of clubs. It looks like two off since there are just four obvious losers, but you will have to watch that the club force does not cause you to lose control. After ruffing the first trick you lead the queen of spades on which West plays the six and East the king. East returns the nine of hearts to his partner's king, and West cashes the ace of hearts before forcing you with another club. How do you plan the play?

It is clear that West began with six clubs and five hearts. He has already produced one spade, and if he has another spade you need not worry too much for he will be cold for six clubs. It is more likely from the bidding, however, that West has a 1–5–1–6 shape. In that case his limit will be eleven tricks in clubs and you will show a loss on the hand if the penalty is more than 300. And it will do you no good to bawl North out for his raise if he is able to point out how you should have escaped for two off.

Four diamond tricks will be available if West has a singleton, and you also have a heart trick to cash. That means you need four trump tricks to bring your tally up to nine, and your only chance is to bring off a trump coup against East. After ruffing the second club you should play your low diamond to the nine, cash the queen of hearts for a diamond discard, and return to hand with a diamond. Now ruff a master diamond in dummy, ruff a club in hand, and ruff another top diamond on the table. At this stage there are only two cards left in each hand, and the play of the last club from dummy enables you to score the jack of spades *en passant*.

The complete deal:

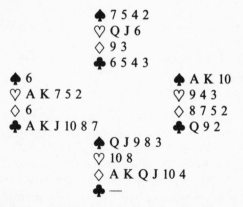

```
                  ♠ 7 5 4 2
                  ♡ Q J 6
                  ◇ 9 3
                  ♣ 6 5 4 3
    ♠ 6                            ♠ A K 10
    ♡ A K 7 5 2                    ♡ 9 4 3
    ◇ 6                            ◇ 8 7 5 2
    ♣ A K J 10 8 7                 ♣ Q 9 2
                  ♠ Q J 9 8 3
                  ♡ 10 8
                  ◇ A K Q J 10 4
                  ♣ —
```

The slightest variation in the timing of the play leads to minus 500 and a poor result.

Are you in a suitable state of relaxed watchfulness by now? Then perhaps you are ready for a tough defensive problem.

```
                    ♠ 6 4
                    ♡ A K 5
                    ◇ A Q J
                    ♣ A K 6 5 2
        ♠ K Q J 10 3
        ♡ 3
        ◇ 7 5 4                      N–S game.
        ♣ Q J 9 7                    Dealer North.
```

West	North	East	South
—	1♣	1♡	pass
1♠	dble	pass	2◇
pass	2♡	pass	2NT
pass	3NT	pass	pass
pass			

You lead the king of spades on which East plays the two and South the seven. How do you plan the defence?

The spades appear to be 3–3 and it looks as though you have made a good start by attacking declarer's entry to his long diamonds. On the bidding South is likely to have five diamonds, but he can hardly have the king of diamonds as well as the ace of spades since he failed to bid on the first round. Besides, East needs a high card on the side to account for his overcall of one heart, and it can only be the king of diamonds. The most probable shape for East is 3–6–2–2. By continuing the spade attack you can take out declarer's ace, forcing him to use his entry before the diamonds can be unblocked. He will then be restricted to two diamond tricks.

Or will he? It is easy to overlook the subsidiary danger. South's bidding suggests that he may hold a half-stopper in hearts, something like J x x. He may be able to create a second entry to his hand by discarding a top heart from dummy as he wins the ace of spades on the third round. He would then be able to engineer an end-play against East, playing the ace and queen of diamonds, winning the club return and cashing the other top club, unblocking the jack of diamonds, and then playing king and another heart to ensure access to his long diamonds. This is the distribution that you have to guard against:

```
                  ♠ 6 4
                  ♡ A K 5
                  ◇ A Q J
                  ♣ A K 6 5 2
  ♠ K Q J 10 3              ♠ 8 5 2
  ♡ 3                       ♡ Q 10 9 8 6 2
  ◇ 7 5 4                   ◇ K 6
  ♣ Q J 9 7                 ♣ 10 4
                  ♠ A 9 7
                  ♡ J 7 4
                  ◇ 10 9 8 3 2
                  ♣ 8 3
```

So it will not do to play a third round of spades. Suppose you switch when your second spade is allowed to win. No, that's no good. Declarer would cash dummy's tops in the minors and then play the queen of diamonds, catching East in a similar end-play. East could avoid the lead by ditching his king of diamonds under the ace, but declarer would then be able to change direction. After cashing the minor suit winners and a top heart, he would exit with a club. You could cash two club winners but would then have to yield the rest of the tricks to South.

All right. What about switching to the queen of clubs at trick two? No, that doesn't work either. Declarer would play a second spade himself and duck it to you, leaving the position essentially the same as before.

The way to protect partner from the damaging end play is to switch to a diamond at trick two. Now you have an answer to anything declarer may try. If he takes the ace of diamonds and ducks a spade, you win and play a diamond to the king. East can exit with a club, leaving South with no way of making more than eight tricks. If South lets the king of diamonds win at trick two, partner switches back to a spade, and if declarer ducks you can switch to clubs yourself.

Is this defence too hard to find? Instinct seems to call for a spade continuation, certainly, and you would have to be on the ball to realize that there is a more urgent job to be done. The spades can always wait.

The contract is also defeated, in a strange sort of way, by a heart switch at trick two. Declarer wins in dummy and can do no better than duck a spade into your hand. But now you can safely continue with a third spade. This is the position:

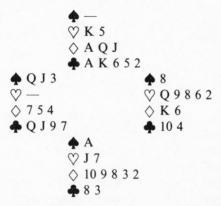

```
                    ♠ —
                    ♡ K 5
                    ◇ A Q J
                    ♣ A K 6 5 2
    ♠ Q J 3                         ♠ 8
    ♡ —                             ♡ Q 9 8 6 2
    ◇ 7 5 4                         ◇ K 6
    ♣ Q J 9 7                       ♣ 10 4
                    ♠ A
                    ♡ J 7
                    ◇ 10 9 8 3 2
                    ♣ 8 3
```

If South discards the king of hearts on the third spade, he can continue by cashing the top clubs and playing ace and queen of diamonds. But now East can escape the trap by returning a low heart, thus preventing the unblocking of the diamonds. If instead South discards the jack of diamonds on the ace of spades and continues with the top clubs and the ace of diamonds, East avoids all problems by dropping the king of diamonds under the ace.

Chapter 5

EXAMINING MOTIVES

The expert has an enquiring mind that is fuelled in part by an enormous mistrust of human nature. He likes to know not only what is going on at the bridge table but exactly why. If an opponent makes an unusual play against him, the master player tends to suspect his opponent's motives rather than his sanity. He knows full well that no opponent is out to do him any favours. 'Why did he do that?' he will ask himself. 'What is he after?' And usually, because of his long experience in the game, he will come up with the right answer.

This spooky business of crawling inside an opponent's skull to examine his innermost thoughts comes more naturally to some than to others, but all experts cultivate the habit to a greater or lesser degree. Those who are strong in psychology exult in the sense of power that comes from reading their opponents' minds as well as the cards. It certainly makes for a strange sort of intimacy when you start probing delicately into the workings of another person's brain.

An obvious occasion for suspicion is when the opponents appear to go out of their way to be helpful. When you are given the opportunity of making a play that you would have been unable to make without the co-operation of the enemy, it behoves you to be particularly careful. Usually it means that the offered option will fail and that the winning line is the one you would have been forced to adopt in the absence of such 'helpful' defence.

Here is a simple example:

```
              ♠ 9 7 4
              ♡ K 7 2
              ◇ 10 8 5
              ♣ Q J 6 5

              ♠ A K 6
              ♡ 5
N–S game.     ◇ A J 9
Dealer South. ♣ A 10 9 8 4 3
```

South	*West*	*North*	*East*
1♣	1♡	2♣	2♡
5♣	pass	pass	pass

West leads the ace of hearts on which East plays the nine. You see that partner's raise was not the world's strongest and you can count four possible losers—a heart, a trump and two diamonds. West continues with the queen of hearts to dummy's king and you discard the six of spades from hand. How do you plan the play?

On the face of it you appear to need to find East with the king of clubs and one of the diamond honours, which is far from impossible on the bidding. However, there is something about the play that does not quite add up. East gave his partner a count of the heart suit on the first round, yet West continued with a second heart to put dummy on lead. Why should he do that? He could see that you had no outside entries to the table, and he would surely not have given you the opportunity to take the trump finesse if it had been right for you.

Without the help of West you would have had no choice but to play the ace of clubs on the first round in the hope of dropping the king. You can discount the possibility that West has taken a sudden liking to you or that he has temporarily lost his reason. The only logical explanation for his play is that he holds the singleton king of clubs. That would provide him with a powerful reason for giving you the chance to take the trump finesse.

You should therefore play a club to your ace at trick three and disconcert West by calling for the king.

The complete deal:

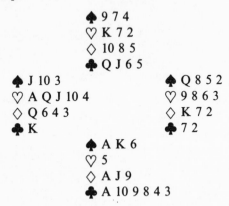

After dropping the king of clubs you can draw a second round of trumps and take two finesses in diamonds to make your contract.

Actually it is superior to ruff a heart at trick three before cashing the ace of clubs. When the king drops, you can cash the ace and king of spades (safe since West can hardly have started with six cards in the suit), cross to the queen of clubs, and ruff the third spade. A club to the jack puts you back in dummy, and now you have a sure end play when you finesse in diamonds, even if both honours are offside.

When an opponent adopts a certain line of play, it is often helpful to consider the alternatives that were available to him and to try to work out why he rejected them.

♠ K 7 6 2
♡ K J 6 4
◇ J 5 2
♣ 8 4

♠ A 9 8 5 3
♡ 10 5 2
N–S game. ◇ A K Q
Dealer South. ♣ A 10

South	West	North	East
1♠	2♣	2♠	pass
4♠	pass	pass	pass

West leads the king of clubs, East plays the two and you win the trick with the ace. Both defenders follow suit when you play a spade to dummy's king, but West shows out, discarding a club, when you win the next spade with your ace. After three rounds of diamonds to which both defenders follow, you exit with the ten of clubs.

West gives his next move a little thought and then plays another club. You ruff in dummy, discarding a heart from hand, and continue with a spade to East's queen. East returns the thirteenth diamond which you ruff in hand. When you play a heart from hand West follows with a low card. Now your moment of decision has arrived. Do you put up the jack or the king?

On the face of it you appear to have a fifty-fifty guess, but in reality there is no guess at all. The expert plays the jack of hearts without apparent thought and claims his contract.

The vital clue to the winning play is West's unusual decision to offer you a ruff and discard when he was in with the second round of clubs. Knowing from his partner's carding that you had three hearts, he would never have done that if he had held the ace of hearts. He would have attacked with a low heart, hoping to find his partner with the queen.

If West had returned a heart you would have had no choice but to play him for the queen. The fact that he rejected the heart play indicates that he wants to provide you with a losing option. You must reject the extra option he is offering and play him for the queen anyway.

The complete deal:

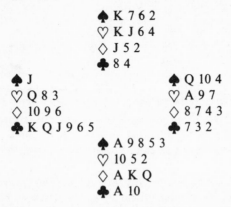

Although it would have made no difference to the result in this particular case, West should really have returned a heart anyway instead of giving you the ruff and discard. That would have brought in two heart tricks for the defence if his partner had held the ten of hearts as well as the ace.

For a change we shall start with all four hands in the next example.

♠ A J 10 6 3
♡ A J 10 4
◇ Q 7
♣ Q 6

♠ K 9 8 5 2   ♠ Q 7
♡ Q 9 3   ♡ 8 6 2
◇ 4 3   ◇ 9 8 6
♣ J 5 2   ♣ A 10 9 4 3

♠ 4
♡ K 7 5
◇ A K J 10 5 2
♣ K 8 7

Game all.
Dealer South.

South	West	North	East
1◇	pass	1♠	pass
3◇	pass	3♡	pass
3NT	pass	4◇	pass
4NT	pass	5♡	pass
6◇	pass	pass	pass

West makes the passive lead of a trump against the diamond slam. Declarer wins in hand, plays a spade to dummy's ace, ruffs a spade in hand, and then plays a club to the two, queen and ace.

Consider the defence from East's point of view. He can count declarer for six diamonds, three clubs according to West's carding, a singleton spade, and therefore three hearts. If East makes the natural return of a trump, declarer will win in dummy, ruff another spade and draw the last trump. In view of the unfriendly spade break declarer will need four tricks from the heart suit, and East can see all too clearly that declarer's only possible way of trying for four heart tricks will be successful, even if West has the queen.

An expert East might therefore reject the trump return and play another club, allowing declarer to take a club ruff in dummy if he needs it. After ruffing the third club on the table, ruffing another spade in hand and drawing the remaining trumps, South reaches the following position:

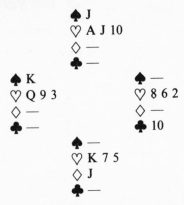

The difference is that South now needs only three heart tricks and there is a two-way finessing position. Declarer can be fairly sure that the hearts are 3–3 and he may finesse the wrong way, taking the view that there is nothing to guide him.

South will get it right, of course, if it occurs to him to wonder why East was so helpful as to allow a club ruff in dummy. Holding Qxx in hearts East could have been virtually certain of defeating the contract by returning a trump, and without doubt he would have done so.

Exploring enemy motives is an activity that can pay dividends for the defenders as well. Whenever declarer makes a play that is in any way out of the ordinary the defenders should ask themselves what is going on. When you have worked out what declarer wants you to do it is often just a matter of doing the opposite.

Here is an example.

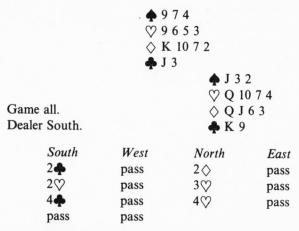

Game all.
Dealer South.

South	West	North	East
2♣	pass	2♦	pass
2♥	pass	3♥	pass
4♣	pass	4♥	pass
pass	pass		

West leads the nine of diamonds against the four-heart contract. Declarer plays low from dummy and wins in hand with the ace, then he cashes the ace of hearts on which partner discards the four of diamonds. South's next move is to play the queen of clubs from hand. Partner follows with the two and the three is played from the table. Over to you.

It seems natural enough to win the trick with the king; indeed, if you don't take the king of clubs now you may never score a club trick. And yet, why has declarer tackled the clubs in this strange way? The bidding makes it plain that he has the ace of clubs, and it would surely have been more natural for him to lead the jack from dummy for a finesse.

The only possible explanation is that declarer has no way of entering dummy except in the club suit. His ace of diamonds must be a singleton, and he is desperate to gain access to dummy so that he can take a discard on the king of diamonds and then finesse against your trumps. If you take your king of clubs, the club jack will serve as his entry. Well, you can put a stop to that idea simply by refusing to take your king. The trick that you give up is sure to come back in one way or another.

The complete deal:

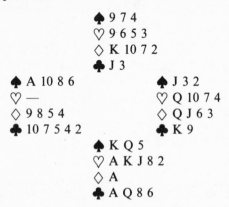

```
              ♠ 9 7 4
              ♡ 9 6 5 3
              ◇ K 10 7 2
              ♣ J 3
♠ A 10 8 6                    ♠ J 3 2
♡ —                          ♡ Q 10 7 4
◇ 9 8 5 4                    ◇ Q J 6 3
♣ 10 7 5 4 2                 ♣ K 9
              ♠ K Q 5
              ♡ A K J 8 2
              ◇ A
              ♣ A Q 8 6
```

Analysis shows that there is no further defence if the first club is won by the king. East may continue with a spade to the king and ace, but South will win the next spade, cross to dummy with the jack of clubs, discard his spade loser on the king of diamonds and draw two further rounds of trumps, finessing against East's queen. South can then revert to clubs, ruffing his loser in dummy. East may overruff, but the defenders score only one club, one spade and one trump.

The difference when East allows the queen of clubs to win is that declarer can never get into dummy to cash the king of diamonds. East is in a position to overruff dummy at every stage and declarer has no escape from four losers.

Instead of leading the queen of clubs South might have tried the play of a low club to dummy's jack. Now East can take his king and switch to spades. South will win the second round of spades and play ace and queen of clubs, discarding the third spade from dummy and putting East to a further test. As long as East refuses to ruff, discarding a spade like dummy, the contract is bound to be defeated. As soon as declarer ruffs something in dummy, East can overruff and return a high trump, leaving declarer with a further loser.

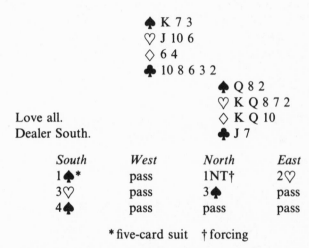

♠ K 7 3
♡ J 10 6
◇ 6 4
♣ 10 8 6 3 2

♠ Q 8 2
♡ K Q 8 7 2
◇ K Q 10
♣ J 7

Love all.
Dealer South.

South	West	North	East
1♠*	pass	1NT†	2♡
3♡	pass	3♠	pass
4♠	pass	pass	pass

* five-card suit   † forcing

West leads the five of hearts to the ten, queen and ace. South cashes the ace of spades and continues with the four of spades to dummy's king, West following with the five and the ten. A club is led from dummy to declarer's queen. Partner produces the king of clubs and leads the nine of hearts, on which the six is played from dummy. What do you make of the situation?

First of all, why did declarer reject the trump finesse which would have succeeded? Clearly because, with only one entry card in dummy, he thought he could best combine his chances by trying to drop the queen of spades and taking the club finesse. Since both these chances have failed the contract seems destined to go one down. How do you make sure of defeating the game?

Partner's carding indicates a holding of three hearts, so you have only one trick to cash in that suit. You also have a club and a spade, and it is clear that you can establish the setting trick in diamonds. But you need to establish that diamond trick before your trump is knocked out, otherwise you may never score it. The safe defence is to overtake the nine of hearts with your king and switch to diamonds. The fact that you set up a second heart trick for declarer is immaterial, for he cannot reach dummy in time to take advantage of it.

The complete deal:

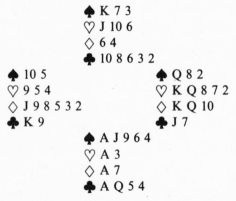

```
              ♠ K 7 3
              ♡ J 10 6
              ◇ 6 4
              ♣ 10 8 6 3 2
♠ 10 5                      ♠ Q 8 2
♡ 9 5 4                     ♡ K Q 8 7 2
◇ J 9 8 5 3 2              ◇ K Q 10
♣ K 9                      ♣ J 7
              ♠ A J 9 6 4
              ♡ A 3
              ◇ A 7
              ♣ A Q 5 4
```

This hand was defended as described by American expert Kit Woolsey in a Men's Board-a-Match event. His partner, Steve Robinson, would no doubt have found the diamond switch himself if the nine of hearts had been allowed to hold. But the position was clearer to Woolsey in the East seat, and in such situations the expert tries to take pressure off his partner.

The contract would have been made with an overtrick if declarer had taken the trump finesse instead of the club finesse, but that line would have been against the odds.

Also, East would not have been able to afford to play the king of hearts on the second round if declarer had drawn only one round of trumps with the king before taking the losing club finesse. If East overtakes the nine of hearts with the king and switches to diamonds, declarer can win the ace, cash the club ace and exit with his second diamond, and the defenders cannot prevent dummy from gaining the lead to take a trump finesse. Still, that line of play would have contained hazards all of its own, and there is no doubt that declarer took his best chance in playing as he did.

Back to the declarer's seat for the next hand.

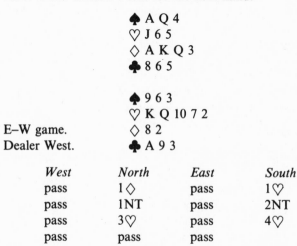

♠ A Q 4
♡ J 6 5
◇ A K Q 3
♣ 8 6 5

♠ 9 6 3
♡ K Q 10 7 2
◇ 8 2
♣ A 9 3

E–W game.
Dealer West.

West	North	East	South
pass	1◇	pass	1♡
pass	1NT	pass	2NT
pass	3♡	pass	4♡
pass	pass	pass	

West leads the queen of clubs and East encourages with the seven. You allow West to hold the first trick, but you take your ace on the next round when he continues with the jack of clubs. There is no point in risking an early ruff by trying to discard a club on the third diamond, since you can always use the diamonds for a spade discard at a later stage. First priority must be given to clearing the trumps, so you play the king of hearts from hand at trick three. East wins with the ace and cashes the king of clubs on which West discards the four of diamonds. East continues with the ten of clubs. How do you play?

Now you have a chance of avoiding the spade finesse altogether.

You could discard a spade from hand and ruff on the table, and once trumps have been drawn your second spade loser would go away on the diamonds. There is a snag, however. West will no doubt discard another diamond on this trick, and your only safe way back to hand after ruffing in dummy will be by overtaking the jack of hearts. That will be fine if the trumps are 3–2 but disastrous if they are 4–1.

And there is, in fact, a strong indication that the trumps *will* break 4–1. Why else would East be so helpful as to offer you a ruff and discard when he could have made a safe trump or diamond return? What is more, on this defence you can be absolutely sure that the spade finesse is working. With the king of spades staring him in the face, East would never offer you a ruff and discard.

You should therefore reject the opportunity to discard a spade from hand on the fourth club. Instead, play a small trump. Whether West overruffs or not you will have no difficulty in drawing the outstanding trumps and making your contract with the help of the spade finesse.

The complete deal:

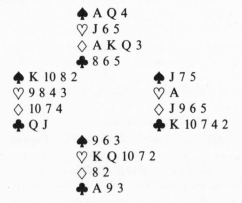

It is clear that East had nothing to lose by offering you the ruff and discard. When a defender does something unorthodox like that, it is important to remember that it indicates that he can see no hope of defeating the contract on a more normal defence.

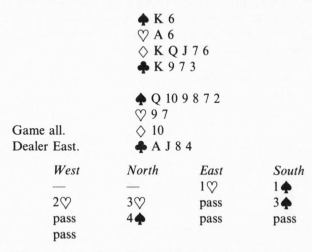

♠ K 6
♡ A 6
◇ K Q J 7 6
♣ K 9 7 3

♠ Q 10 9 8 7 2
♡ 9 7
◇ 10
♣ A J 8 4

Game all.
Dealer East.

West	North	East	South
—	—	1♡	1♠
2♡	3♡	pass	3♠
pass	4♠	pass	pass
pass			

West leads the five of hearts to dummy's ace, and at trick two you play a low diamond from the table. East takes his ace, cashes the queen of hearts on which West plays the eight, and continues with a third heart. How do you plan the play?

The problem here is to pick up the jack of spades. East's line of defence—knowingly conceding a ruff and discard—suggests that he is aware that further defensive tricks can come only from the trump suit. If the hearts are 6–3 he may be planning to lead a further heart when he is in with the ace of spades in the hope of promoting something for his partner.

Clearly it will not do to ruff this heart in dummy, for then you will succeed only if East has A J doubleton in spades. On balance it seems likely that the jack will be with West twice guarded and that East will have the doubleton ace. What about ruffing in hand and running the ten of spades? That will be fine if East takes his ace, but his play will be to hold off, win the second spade, and then lead

another heart to promote his partner's jack of spades. The only
way to counter this threat is by a trump reduction play, and for
that you will need an extra entry to dummy. You must therefore
ruff the third heart with a middle spade and then lead the two of
spades to dummy's six. The king of hearts appears from West on
the third round, and the complete deal is:

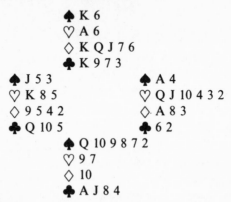

```
                    ♠ K 6
                    ♡ A 6
                    ◇ K Q J 7 6
                    ♣ K 9 7 3
      ♠ J 5 3                      ♠ A 4
      ♡ K 8 5                      ♡ Q J 10 4 3 2
      ◇ 9 5 4 2                    ◇ A 8 3
      ♣ Q 10 5                     ♣ 6 2
                    ♠ Q 10 9 8 7 2
                    ♡ 9 7
                    ◇ 10
                    ♣ A J 8 4
```

When East allows the six of spades to hold, you continue with
top diamonds from dummy, discarding two clubs from hand. If
East ruffs the fourth diamond with the ace of spades your troubles
are over. If he discards a club, you ruff in hand, cash the ace of
clubs and continue with a club to the king. If East ruffs this time,
West's jack of spades is smothered on the heart return. And if East
discards, you ruff a club in hand and claim your game-going trick
with Q 10 opposite dummy's king.

It is quite a complicated hand, and it is only by considering
East's motives for offering you a ruff and discard that you can
arrive at the winning line of play.

♠ A 10 2
♡ 5
◇ A K J 7 6 3
♣ 10 8 2

♠ 6
♡ A J 9 3
◇ Q 9 4
♣ A K Q 7 6

N–S game.
Dealer North.

West	North	East	South
—	1◇	pass	3♣
3NT	4◇	4♠	4NT
pass	5♣	pass	7◇
dble	pass	pass	7NT
pass	pass	pass	

West's overcall of three notrumps was explained as 'unusual', indicating a major two-suiter. North's 'Byzantine' response of five clubs to your enquiry of four notrumps showed three controls, which you could identify as two aces and the king of diamonds. Seven diamonds therefore seemed a sound proposition, but when West produced his Lightner double you decided that seven notrumps might prove a safer spot.

West leads the king of hearts to your ace. How do you plan the play?

Having just eleven top tricks, you need to develop two more. Since West with his Lightner double announced his ability to ruff a club, the two extra tricks could both come from clubs. Alternatively, you could be content to develop one extra club trick and rely on a double squeeze for the thirteenth trick. The latter is by far the better method and has a special appeal for those with suspicious minds.

After winning the ace of hearts you should cash the ace of clubs, unblocking the eight from the table when West shows out as expected. The queen of diamonds is followed by a diamond to dummy's jack, and the ten of clubs is led to force a cover from East (not that it matters if he refuses to cover). You capture the jack of clubs with your queen and run the rest of the diamonds. On the play of the last diamond East will have to come down to a singleton spade in order to keep three clubs. You can then discard a club from hand on the last diamond, finesse the seven of clubs, and cash the club king to squeeze West in the majors.

Why not avoid all this fancy work by running the ten of clubs on the first round, did someone say? A glance at the complete deal provides the answer.

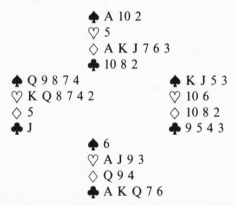

```
                    ♠ A 10 2
                    ♡ 5
                    ◇ A K J 7 6 3
                    ♣ 10 8 2
   ♠ Q 9 8 7 4                      ♠ K J 5 3
   ♡ K Q 8 7 4 2                    ♡ 10 6
   ◇ 5                              ◇ 10 8 2
   ♣ J                              ♣ 9 5 4 3
                    ♠ 6
                    ♡ A J 9 3
                    ◇ Q 9 4
                    ♣ A K Q 7 6
```

West's psychic Lightner double was a brilliant attempt to lead you astray. But in this particular case there is no need to allow him to shine at your expense.

Chapter 6

INDUCING ERROR

The expert is not content with keeping his own game reasonably free from error. A significant part of his attention is constantly directed towards inducing error in his opponents. This is particularly the case when he is facing opponents of his own calibre. Taking the view that his fellow experts play far too well when left in peace to get on with it, he refuses to leave them in peace but harries them continually with bluff leads, false cards, and assorted deceptive manoeuvres designed to suggest that the winning line of play is in fact the losing one and vice versa.

Expert opponents, who tend to rely heavily on obtaining an accurate count of the hand, are especially vulnerable to delicate false-carding which may induce a miscount. The picture must not be painted with too heavy a brush, naturally. And subtlety is wasted, of course, on players who will not notice a false card when it stares them in the face.

Adept at concealing the strengths and weaknesses of his hand, the expert often surprises opponents by turning up with unexpected winners in the later play. The art of misdirection is a delicate one. A master player may be able to paint a false picture of his values and suggest a losing defence simply by adopting a slightly off-beat line of play.

Sometimes all that is required is to put the defenders to the test at the earliest possible moment. A good player is much more easily persuaded to do the wrong thing early in the play than in the later stages when most of the hand is an open book.

Here is a simple example:

```
                    ♠ 10 8 7 5 2
                    ♡ K Q 4
                    ◇ K J 10 5 4
                    ♣ —

                    ♠ K Q 9 4
                    ♡ A 9 3
Game all.           ◇ Q 9 6 3
Dealer West.        ♣ 7 5
```

West	North	East	South
pass	pass	1♣	pass
1♡	dble	2♣	2♠
3♣	4♠	5♣	5♠
dble	pass	pass	pass

West leads the three of clubs and dummy is a pleasant sight. You bid five spades as a sacrifice but—who knows?—you may end up by making the contract. Ruffing the club lead in dummy, you play the five of spades. East puts in the three and your king wins, West dropping the six. How should you continue?

It looks as though you may have to lose only one trump trick, but you need to play the second round of trumps from dummy in case East started with A J 3. It seems natural to enter dummy by ruffing your second club. To be sure, you may get away with this if the diamonds are 2–2, but your thinking should be directed at this point towards the danger of a 3–1 diamond break. If East has A J 3 of spades and a singleton diamond, he is not going to play low on the second round of spades. He will rise with the ace, play the diamond to his partner's ace and ruff the diamond return to put you one down.

The expert way of entering dummy at trick three—and the safest way, strangely enough—is to grasp the nettle by leading a

diamond, preferably the nine. It is hard for West, holding A x x in
diamonds, to judge the correct play. By going up with the ace he
may be making it possible for you to drop his partner's queen on
the next round for all he knows. If East plays low on the diamond
lead, you win in dummy and play another spade secure in the
knowledge that the danger of a diamond ruff has disappeared.

The complete deal:

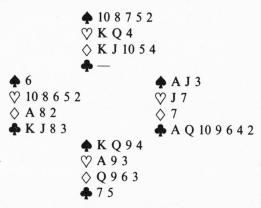

♠ 10 8 7 5 2
♡ K Q 4
◇ K J 10 5 4
♣ —

♠ 6
♡ 10 8 6 5 2
◇ A 8 2
♣ K J 8 3

♠ A J 3
♡ J 7
◇ 7
♣ A Q 10 9 6 4 2

♠ K Q 9 4
♡ A 9 3
◇ Q 9 6 3
♣ 7 5

East may win the next spade but he has no way of putting West
on lead to give him the diamond ruff.

You are assured of a good score even if you go one down since
five clubs is a make for East and West. But how much better to
make your contract!

Both defenders had the chance to defeat you, East by going up
with the ace of spades on the first round and switching to
diamonds, and West by taking his diamond ace and continuing the
suit. Neither play was at all obvious.

The next deal has points of interest for both sides. Let's show all
four hands and tackle the problem from declarer's seat first.

```
                      ♠ Q 5
                      ♡ 9 7 6 3
                      ◇ Q J 8 4
                      ♣ 8 6 5
         ♠ J 10 9 6              ♠ 8 7 4 3 2
         ♡ J 8 4 2              ♡ 10 5
         ◇ 10 6 3               ◇ K 7 2
         ♣ J 4                  ♣ K Q 10
                      ♠ A K
                      ♡ A K Q
Love all.             ◇ A 9 5
Dealer South.         ♣ A 9 7 3 2
```

South	West	North	East
2♣	pass	2◇	pass
2NT	pass	3♣	pass
3◇	pass	3NT	pass
pass	pass		

West leads the jack of spades, hitting declarer in the weak spot and denying him the tempo to establish the club suit. Declarer's first move, naturally, is to test the hearts by cashing the ace, king and queen. If the hearts split 3–3 he can make the game easily enough by establishing one extra trick in diamonds.

East discards a spade on the third round of hearts, however, and South has to think again. He now needs three tricks from the diamond suit to make his contract. A straightforward method of play would be to cash the ace of diamonds and continue with the nine to dummy's jack. That would bring in three diamond tricks if either defender had the king doubleton. If West had that holding the king would pop up on the second round, while if East produced the king on the second round South could take a later finesse against the ten of diamonds. This play will fail when the diamonds are 3–3, however, since the defender with the king will hold it up until the third round.

A more subtle line of play works not only when the king is doubleton but also in some of the 3–3 breaks as well. The expert play is to lead the five of diamonds from hand and insert dummy's eight if West plays low. As the cards lie, this places East in an impossible dilemma. He can either take his king of diamonds on the first round, thereby allowing South to score three diamond tricks, or he can hold up. In the latter event South can continue with the queen of diamonds from dummy, finessing against the king and making three diamond tricks anyway. All very satisfying from declarer's point of view.

It was mentioned that this line of play would also succeed against a doubleton king on either side. That is because West, holding K x, is virtually certain to play the king when declarer leads the five from hand. But what if he doesn't? Suppose the cards are divided as shown below.

If West bravely plays low when the five of diamonds is led, he prepares the way for the defeat of the contract. East has to play his part by withholding his ten when the eight is finessed. Declarer naturally assumes that he has struck the defensive holdings shown on the previous page and runs the queen of diamonds on the way back. West produces the king, and with the diamonds blocked declarer can make no more than eight tricks. All very satisfactory from the defenders' point of view.

It would be far from easy to achieve the degree of co-operation needed to bring off such a defence but it would not be impossible in

an expert game. West can see that there is no future for the defence
if he wins the first diamond with the king, and East for his part
knows that on declarer's line of play his partner must have a
doubleton diamond honour. One further short step may enable
East to envisage the actual position where partner holds the king.
Imagination is a great asset when it comes to creating illusions in
the minds of opponents. As a corollary, it is imaginative players
who are the most easily deceived.

You will need to exercise some imagination to whistle up a
chance of making game on the next hand.

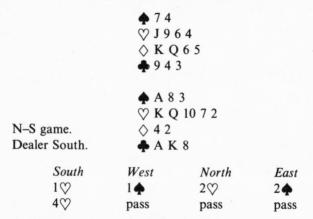

	♠ 7 4
	♡ J 9 6 4
	◇ K Q 6 5
	♣ 9 4 3

	♠ A 8 3
	♡ K Q 10 7 2
N–S game.	◇ 4 2
Dealer South.	♣ A K 8

South	West	North	East
1♡	1♠	2♡	2♠
4♡	pass	pass	pass

West leads the jack of diamonds. How do you plan the play?

Prospects are bleak, since East is marked with the ace of
diamonds on this lead. East is not likely to be 5–5 in the minors,
and even if he is the defenders will not allow you to set up a minor-
suit squeeze. It is hard to see any way of avoiding a loser in each
suit.

Against weak opposition you would have no chance at all, but if
East is a strong and imaginative defender there is a faint hope. Try
the effect of playing low from dummy to the first trick!

The complete deal:

♠ 7 4
♡ J 9 6 4
◇ K Q 6 5
♣ 9 4 3

♠ K J 10 6 2   ♠ Q 9 5
♡ A 3   ♡ 8 5
◇ J 10   ◇ A 9 8 7 3
♣ Q 10 6 2   ♣ J 7 5

♠ A 8 3
♡ K Q 10 7 2
◇ 4 2
♣ A K 8

Look at the matter from East's point of view. He is bound to regard your play of a low diamond from dummy with grave suspicion. It will appear to him that you can hold no more than one diamond and that you are desperate to keep him off lead. In an effort to thwart your plan he may therefore overtake his partner's jack of diamonds with the ace and shoot back a spade, expecting the complete deal to be something like this:

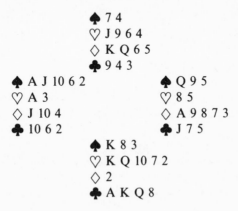

♠ 7 4
♡ J 9 6 4
◇ K Q 6 5
♣ 9 4 3

♠ A J 10 6 2   ♠ Q 9 5
♡ A 3   ♡ 8 5
◇ J 10 4   ◇ A 9 8 7 3
♣ 10 6 2   ♣ J 7 5

♠ K 8 3
♡ K Q 10 7 2
◇ 2
♣ A K Q 8

East's imaginative defence is the only way to defeat the contract if this is the layout. On the actual lie of the cards, of course, he allows you to make the contract.

There are many ways in which the defenders can paint a distorted picture of their holdings for declarer. Good results can often be achieved by parting with an honour card before it is due to fall. Here is an example from an American team event.

```
                    ♠ 6 4
                    ♡ Q J 10 8 3
                    ◇ A Q 6 5
                    ♣ 3 2
    ♠ Q J 10 5 2              ♠ K 9 7
    ♡ 5                       ♡ 7 6 4 2
    ◇ K 10 9 8                ◇ 3 2
    ♣ Q 8 7                   ♣ A J 10 4
                    ♠ A 8 3
                    ♡ A K 9
Game all.           ◇ J 7 4
Dealer South.       ♣ K 9 6 5
```

South	West	North	East
1NT	pass	2◇*	pass
2♡	pass	3◇	pass
3♡	pass	4♡	pass
pass	pass		

*transfer to hearts

South played in the sound contract of four hearts—a contract that is destined to succeed on the lie of the cards. Declarer can score five trump tricks in dummy, one spade, two diamonds and a club, and the tenth trick comes from a diamond ruff in his own hand.

The opening lead of the queen of spades was allowed to hold the first trick. South won the spade continuation, finessed the queen of diamonds and cashed the diamond ace. In the West seat was a young expert, Jeff Meckstroth, who does not believe in submitting meekly to destiny. He stirred the pot by dropping the king of diamonds under the ace. This gave declarer a ninth trick immediately, and South began to wonder if it might be possible to make his contract even if the ace of clubs was in the West hand. He drew two rounds of trumps with the ace and king, and when West discarded a spade on the second round the position seemed clear. Having no more trumps West would be unable to ruff the third round of diamonds, so declarer confidently attempted to cash the jack, intending to continue by ruffing a spade in dummy and ruffing the fourth diamond in hand.

Now the roof fell in, for this was the position:

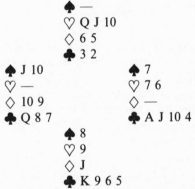

East ruffed the jack of diamonds and returned his last trump, and it was no longer possible for South to make his contract.

Opportunities for artistic misdirection of this sort occur quite frequently. The next example comes from a Gold Cup match.

```
                    ♠ —
                    ♡ 7 6 4
                    ◇ A K J 8 7 4 2
                    ♣ 10 6 3
        ♠ J 7                     ♠ Q 5 4 2
        ♡ K 10 8 2                ♡ Q J 3
        ◇ Q 9 3                   ◇ 6 5
        ♣ J 9 7 5                 ♣ A Q 8 2
                    ♠ A K 10 9 8 6 3
                    ♡ A 9 5
Game all.           ◇ 10
Dealer South.       ♣ K 4
```

South	West	North	East
2♠	pass	3◇	pass
3♣	pass	4◇	pass
4♠	pass	pass	pass

South played in four spades and received the lead of the two of hearts. He won the first trick with the ace of hearts, cashed the ace and king of spades, and then played the ace and king of diamonds, discarding a heart from hand. He intended to continue with a club towards his king, a play which would have brought in ten tricks.

On the second round of diamonds, however, West dropped the queen! Now it seemed safe for South to cash the jack of diamonds for a further heart discard. If West were able to ruff it would surely be with the queen of spades, since he had played the jack on the second round of trumps, and the only losers would be a trump and two clubs.

But, to South's chagrin, it was East who ruffed the third diamond with the five of spades. South was able to overruff and play a heart, but East won this trick, cashed his master spade and exited with his third heart. South eventually had to play clubs from his own hand and could not avoid defeat.

Sometimes the chance to point declarer in the wrong direction is recognized only in the post-mortem. Here is another hand from a Gold Cup match.

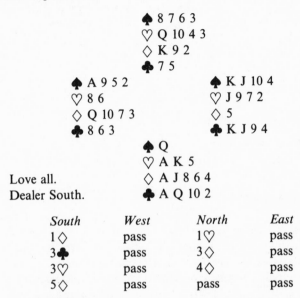

```
                    ♠ 8 7 6 3
                    ♡ Q 10 4 3
                    ◇ K 9 2
                    ♣ 7 5
    ♠ A 9 5 2                      ♠ K J 10 4
    ♡ 8 6                          ♡ J 9 7 2
    ◇ Q 10 7 3                     ◇ 5
    ♣ 8 6 3                        ♣ K J 9 4
                    ♠ Q
                    ♡ A K 5
    Love all.       ◇ A J 8 6 4
    Dealer South.   ♣ A Q 10 2
```

South	West	North	East
1◇	pass	1♡	pass
3♣	pass	3◇	pass
3♡	pass	4◇	pass
5◇	pass	pass	pass

West began with the ace and another spade. Ruffing the second spade, South played a heart to dummy's queen, finessed the queen of clubs, cashed the club ace and ruffed the two of clubs in dummy. He returned to hand with the king of hearts and led his fourth club. West could not gain by ruffing, so he discarded a spade and dummy ruffed with the diamond nine. The king of diamonds was cashed, a spade was ruffed, and then the play of the ace of hearts forced West to ruff and return a trump into South's tenace.

South played well to make his eleven tricks, certainly, but East was already kicking himself for missing a great opportunity. Suppose that on the second and third rounds of clubs East had played the jack and the king!

This would have been the position with dummy on lead:

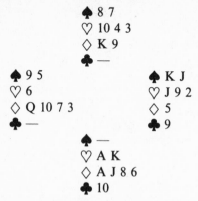

♠ 8 7
♡ 10 4 3
◇ K 9
♣ —

♠ 9 5   ♠ K J
♡ 6   ♡ J 9 2
◇ Q 10 7 3   ◇ 5
♣ —   ♣ 9

♠ —
♡ A K
◇ A J 8 6
♣ 10

With his ten of clubs established as a winner, do you think that declarer would have continued in the same way? It is highly improbable, for he would not wish to run the risk of an overruff by East on the fourth round of clubs. Having no further losers in the side suits, declarer would surely have played the king and another trump, hoping to find a 3–2 split. And that, on the lie of the cards, would have resulted in one down.

Here is a hand from the American Life Masters Pairs where the declarer was caught in a web of deception.

♠ 10 8
♡ A J 9 7
◇ A K 9 8 4
♣ J 8

♠ Q 9 6 4   ♠ A J 7 3
♡ Q 8 6 5   ♡ 10 4 3
◇ Q J   ◇ 10 7 6 5 3
♣ Q 9 7   ♣ 4

♠ K 5 2
♡ K 2
Game all.   ◇ 2
Dealer East.   ♣ A K 10 6 5 3 2

West	North	East	South
—	—	pass	1♣
pass	1◇	pass	2♣
pass	2♡	pass	2NT
pass	3NT	pass	pass
pass			

The defenders were two prominent American experts, Andy Bernstein, West, and Mike Becker, East. Bernstein led the four of spades to his partner's ace. Instead of returning the normal 'fourth-highest' three of spades, Becker returned the jack. After all, declarer might have held the queen of spades and West the king and nine. When the jack was allowed to win the trick East continued with the seven of spades to South's king. Although the play of the jack had not trapped the queen in the South hand, it succeeded in giving South a false picture of the distribution. South knew that someone was concealing the three of spades and it seemed to him that it was more likely to be West than East.

After winning the spade king South cashed the ace of clubs, unblocking the jack from dummy, and crossed to the table with the king of diamonds, noting West's jack. A club to the king came next and declarer, believing West to have started with a five-card spade suit, did not dare to play another club. Instead he cashed the king of hearts, finessed dummy's jack of hearts and continued with the ace. Everyone was down to four cards and this is what declarer imagined the end position to be:

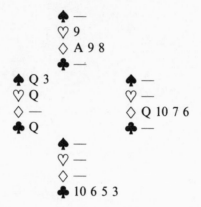

South played the eight of diamonds from the table, confident that East would have to concede two diamond tricks on his return. Of course the actual position was the following:

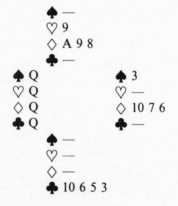

West was happy to claim the rest of the tricks with his four queens.

The value of offering the declarer a losing option is illustrated in striking fashion by this hand from the French international trials of 1977.

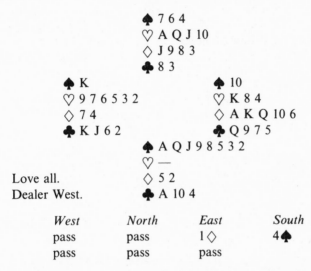

♠ 7 6 4
♡ A Q J 10
◇ J 9 8 3
♣ 8 3

♠ K
♡ 9 7 6 5 3 2
◇ 7 4
♣ K J 6 2

♠ 10
♡ K 8 4
◇ A K Q 10 6
♣ Q 9 7 5

♠ A Q J 9 8 5 3 2
♡ —
◇ 5 2
♣ A 10 4

Love all.
Dealer West.

West	North	East	South
pass	pass	1◇	4♠
pass	pass	pass	

In one room the defenders were Dominique Pilon and Pierre Jais. Pilon led a diamond to his partner's ten. Jais cashed the ace of diamonds and continued with the king, which was ruffed by declarer with the nine of spades. (Why not with the jack, I wonder?)

Resisting the impulse to seize the chance of making his king of spades, Pilon calmly discarded a club on this trick. It then seemed to declarer that he could afford to play the ace and another club, subsequently ruffing the third club in dummy and taking the marked trump finesse to land his contract. Jais won the second club and played another diamond, however, and this time Pilon took his king of spades to put the contract one down.

The contract was the same in the other room and the defence started on similar lines, but West overruffed the third diamond and returned a club to declarer's ace. On this defence, the only option available to South was a winning one. He drew the outstanding trump with the ace, crossed to dummy with a second trump, discarded a club on the ace of hearts and continued with the heart queen. When East played low, South discarded his remaining club and claimed ten tricks.

For a final example of making life difficult for the opponents, watch Per-Olov Sundelin of Sweden in action on this hand from the *Sunday Times* Tournament of 1980.

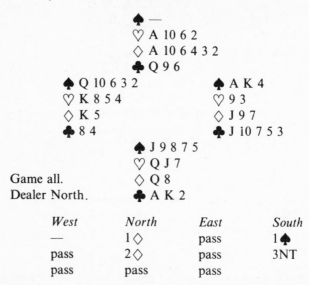

```
                    ♠ —
                    ♡ A 10 6 2
                    ◇ A 10 6 4 3 2
                    ♣ Q 9 6
        ♠ Q 10 6 3 2              ♠ A K 4
        ♡ K 8 5 4                 ♡ 9 3
        ◇ K 5                     ◇ J 9 7
        ♣ 8 4                     ♣ J 10 7 5 3
                    ♠ J 9 8 7 5
                    ♡ Q J 7
Game all.           ◇ Q 8
Dealer North.       ♣ A K 2
```

West	North	East	South
—	1◇	pass	1♠
pass	2◇	pass	3NT
pass	pass	pass	

West led the four of hearts to the two, nine and queen. Sundelin saw that his partner's light opening bid had landed them in game on rather thin values. Judging correctly that the chances were poor of establishing the diamond suit for the loss of only one trick and at the same time avoiding four losers in spades, he decided to tackle the spade suit himself. This would give him some technical chances. If the spades were 4–4 or if the six dropped in three rounds, for instance, he would be able to establish a spade trick by weight of cards. And it would make it hard for the defenders to fathom what was going on.

At trick two, therefore, Sundelin led the eight of spades from hand. West played low, a diamond was discarded from dummy, and East won with the king. The three of hearts was returned to the seven, eight and ten. Trying to give the impression of a more substantial club holding than he actually held, Sundelin played the nine of clubs from dummy. When East played low, South won with the king and continued with the nine of spades. Again West played low, a diamond was thrown from dummy, and East won with the ace. The position was as follows:

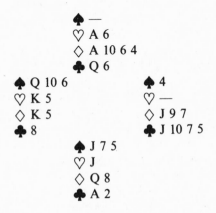

If East returns a club at this point, declarer can win in hand, run the jack of hearts, cross to dummy with the club queen, cash the ace of hearts for a spade discard, and then play ace and another diamond to end-play West.

In practice East decided that South was quite likely to have a singleton diamond. He therefore returned the seven of diamonds, and Sundelin was home when he guessed correctly to play the eight from hand.

The only winning defence in the diagram position is for East to continue with a third spade. After winning a spade trick West can switch to his club, and a throw-in is no longer possible. From East's point of view that might have been the only way of letting the game home, however. All credit to South for obscuring the position.

Chapter 7

WEIGHING THE COMPLETE EVIDENCE

Most of the techniques related to card-reading—counting the hand, drawing inferences about the location of high cards from the bidding, the opening lead and the play, and examining the motives of the opponents—are well within the scope of any good player. What distinguishes the expert, perhaps, is the thoroughness with which he goes about his task.

Before committing himself to any course of action based on an assumption, the expert will consider from every angle the full consequences of that assumption. If he finds anything that is incompatible with the rest of the evidence, he will discard the assumption and look for something else. On certain hands there may be indications that seem to point in opposite directions. Every shred of evidence has to be weighed in the balance and given its due worth before an informed decision can be made.

Once a tentative decision has been made, the expert will still be in no hurry to put it into effect. He will carry out a careful last-minute review of the bidding, the play *and* the opponents, looking for any detail that does not appear to fit into the picture of the unseen hands that he has built up.

This does not mean that the expert huddles interminably over every play. The process of thought may take less than a second to complete. Nevertheless the work has been done, either consciously or subconsciously, and that is why the expert makes few mistakes in these situations.

See if you can manage to take account of every scrap of evidence in the examples that follow.

```
                    ♠ A 4
                    ♡ A 9 8 5 3
                    ◇ Q 4
                    ♣ K Q 9 2


                    ♠ Q 7
                    ♡ 6
Love all.           ◇ A K 8 5 3 2
Dealer North.       ♣ A 10 7 3
```

West	North	East	South
—	1NT	pass	3◇
4♠	pass	pass	5♣
5♡	dble	5♠	pass
pass	6♣	pass	pass
pass			

West leads the two of spades against your slam. How do you plan the play?

It hardly seems likely that West would have jumped to four spades without the king of the suit, and there is a temptation to run the first trick to your queen. You will certainly be well placed if the queen wins. But before you commit yourself to this play there are two questions you should ask yourself. Is it safe? And is it necessary?

To answer the first question you have only to take another look at West's choice of lead—the two of spades from a suit in which he must surely have seven cards. Have the opponents taken to leading seventh highest? Not likely. West's choice of card must be intended as a suit-preference signal asking for a return of the lower-ranking side suit, diamonds. Presumably West is void in diamonds and hopes to ruff the return. This implies that he expects his partner to gain the lead, so the king of spades may well be with East after all.

It is both unsafe and unnecessary to play low from dummy at

trick one. You have five top tricks in the side suits, and if you can manage to score seven trump tricks you will be home. A count of West's hand tells you that seven trump tricks will be available. In addition to his seven spades West must have five hearts (his partner gave preference to spades, remember), which leaves room in his hand for just one trump. So at trick one you go up with the ace of spades, cash the king of clubs and then play on diamonds.

The complete deal:

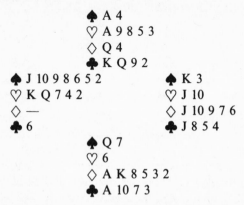

Having extracted West's solitary trump, you play three rounds of diamonds, discarding the spade loser from dummy. Then it is just a simple crossruff—diamond ruff, heart ace, heart ruff, diamond ruff, heart ruff, spade ruff with the queen of trumps and heart ruff with the ace of trumps for your twelfth trick.

Even if West had been less obvious about his desire for a ruff, leading the jack of spades initially instead of the two, you should probably still decide to adopt this line of play.

Now for a defensive problem.

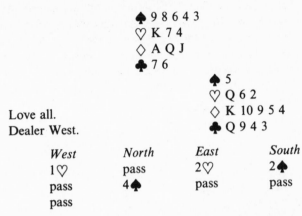

♠ 9 8 6 4 3
♡ K 7 4
◇ A Q J
♣ 7 6

♠ 5
♡ Q 6 2
◇ K 10 9 5 4
♣ Q 9 4 3

Love all.
Dealer West.

West	North	East	South
1♡	pass	2♡	2♠
pass	4♠	pass	pass
pass			

Partner wins the first two tricks with the ace and king of trumps. You discard a low diamond on the second spade, and partner switches to the jack of hearts which runs to declarer's ace. South now leads the six of diamonds to the eight and ace and continues with the queen of diamonds from the table. Quick! What do you do?

Unless you have already played low with the right degree of unconcern you have given away the game. It is one of those situations where you cannot afford to take time to think; the slightest hesitation is bound to be fatal. In any case there is nothing to think about.

You don't really suppose that declarer would tackle the suit like this if he had another diamond in his hand, do you? No, that six of diamonds was clearly a singleton and there can be no point in covering the queen. If declarer needs a discard on the diamonds he is going to take it anyway. But the chances are that declarer doesn't need a discard at all. The most likely explanation for his play is that he is trying to find out where the high cards lie so that he will know how to play the clubs. He is marked with at least four cards in clubs, and that is probably the key suit for him.

The complete deal:

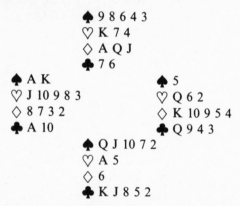

If declarer discovers that you have the king of diamonds his task becomes much easier. Now he can deduce that West must have the ace of clubs to account for his opening bid. After crossing to dummy with the king of hearts and leading a club, therefore, South takes the winning position by putting in his jack.

The position is quite different if you calmly play low on the second round of diamonds. Declarer will probably assume that the king of diamonds is with West, in which case you would need to have the ace of clubs to account for your raise. After ruffing the queen of diamonds, returning to the king of hearts and playing a club, South is likely to misjudge by going up with the king.

Back to declarer's seat for the next hand.

<pre>
              ♠ A 3
              ♡ A 7 4 2
              ◇ 10 9 7 6
              ♣ A 4 3

              ♠ K J 9 8 5 4
              ♡ K 10 5
Game all.   ◇ 8
Dealer East. ♣ K J 2
</pre>

West	North	East	South
—	—	pass	1♠
pass	2♣	2◇	2♠
pass	4♠	pass	pass
pass			

West leads the four of diamonds to his partner's ace. East returns the queen of diamonds and you ruff low, West following with the five. When you play a spade to dummy's ace the queen appears from the West hand. How should you continue?

You need to score six trump tricks to be sure of your contract, and there is a temptation to take a finesse against the ten of spades on the second round. That would be safe enough if West were a beginner, but it is poor play against an experienced defender. Players have been known to drop the queen from Q 10 doubleton. In any case there is a much better way of securing six tricks in trumps.

Ruff another diamond at trick four (West is known to have three diamonds from the carding of both defenders) and then play the king of spades. If West shows out as expected, play a heart to dummy's ace and a heart back to your king, then a club to the ace and a club back to your king. East cannot gain by ruffing a loser if he happens to have a singleton in one of these suits. Once you have secured your four tricks in the side suits you can simply exit with a heart or a club and wait for two further tricks in trumps.

The complete deal:

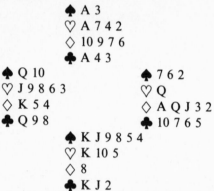

```
                    ♠ A 3
                    ♡ A 7 4 2
                    ◇ 10 9 7 6
                    ♣ A 4 3
    ♠ Q 10                        ♠ 7 6 2
    ♡ J 9 8 6 3                   ♡ Q
    ◇ K 5 4                       ◇ A Q J 3 2
    ♣ Q 9 8                       ♣ 10 7 6 5
                    ♠ K J 9 8 5 4
                    ♡ K 10 5
                    ◇ 8
                    ♣ K J 2
```

West was being clever, right enough. When the ten of spades drops, of course, you can draw the remaining trump and try for an overtrick.

If you had finessed and lost to the ten of spades on the second round of trumps, you might subsequently have recovered by reading the end position correctly and bringing off a throw-in against West. But you might equally well have got it wrong and lost your contract.

♠ A K Q 10 7
♡ J 10 5
◊ Q 5 2
♣ 10 8

♠ 4 3 2
♡ Q 9 6
◊ J 7
♣ A K 4 3 2

Game all.
Dealer North.

West	North	East	South
—	1♠	pass	2♡
pass	2♠	pass	3NT
pass	4♡	pass	pass
pass			

West leads the nine of clubs to your king and South follows with the five. How do you plan the defence?

The lead marks partner with a doubleton club, so you know that you can cash a second trick in the suit. Also there are interesting possibilities for a trump promotion. If partner can ruff the third club high enough to force out one of dummy's trump honours you may enjoy a trump trick with your Q 9 6. Still, that would amount to no more than three tricks for the defence. What about a fourth trick?

On the bidding you can place South with five trumps and West with a doubleton. If West has either the ace or the king of hearts, you will make two trump tricks by weight of cards. If South has both top honours in trumps, partner may have something good in diamonds. You must hope that he has the diamond ace, for otherwise declarer is likely to be able to discard his diamond losers on dummy's spades. Even the ace of diamonds may be lost unless you switch to the suit straight away. Declarer is known to have five hearts and four clubs, and on the bidding he is likely to be 2–2 in the other suits. The spades are breaking, in fact, and if you give him the chance declarer will draw two rounds of trumps and then play four rounds of spades, discarding both of his diamonds.

The right defence must be to play a diamond to West's hypothetical ace at trick two. Then, after a switch back to clubs, you can try the trump-promotion play with a third round of clubs.

The complete deal:

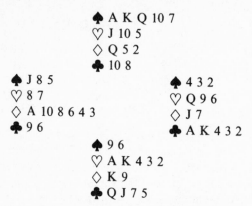

How does partner know to revert to clubs after winning the ace of diamonds? Might he not try to give you a diamond ruff instead? The answer is quite simple and logical. If you had been interested in a diamond ruff you would have won the first trick with the ace of clubs, not the king. Alternatively, you could have cashed both clubs before switching to diamonds.

If you failed to find the right answer to this problem you are in good company. In the final of the 1979 Vanderbilt, one of the most important American team events, both East players got it wrong, playing three rounds of clubs immediately. West's seven of hearts forced out dummy's ten, but the declarers countered with two rounds of trumps and then four rounds of spades, and South's last diamond went away as East ruffed.

Trump management can get very complicated at times.

<pre>
                    ♠ Q 4
                    ♡ 10 8 5 2
                    ◇ 9 7 3 2
                    ♣ A 7 4

                    ♠ K J 10 9 5 3
                    ♡ 4
Game all.   ◇ A K
Dealer South.   ♣ K Q 6 2
</pre>

South	West	North	East
1♠	pass	1NT	pass
4♠	dble	pass	pass
pass			

West leads the ace of hearts on which East plays the queen. The continuation of the three of hearts goes to East's nine and your three of spades. How do you plan the play?

On the face of it there are only three potential losers—a spade, a heart and a club. But West's double has to be explained in some way, and it is hard to avoid the conclusion that he must have all the outstanding trumps. He has only the ace and king of hearts on the side, after all. With West holding five spades, you cannot afford to play even one round of trumps. West would win and force you with another heart, and you would have to lose four tricks.

So you have to consider whether anything can be achieved by playing on the side suits. The hearts appear to be 4–4, and your best hope is that West is 2–2 in the minors. Suppose you cash the top diamonds and continue with ace, king and queen of clubs. No good! West will ruff and counter with the ace and another trump, leaving you with a losing club in your hand. Somehow you must arrange matters so that you have a *winning* club left if West adopts the defence of drawing your trumps.

The only play that can succeed against West's probable 5–4–2–2 pattern is to cash the top diamonds, play the king of clubs and a club to the ace, ruff another heart in hand, and then exit with your low club.

The complete deal:

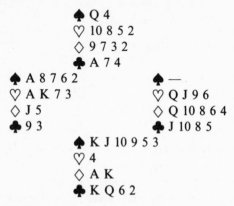

```
                    ♠ Q 4
                    ♡ 10 8 5 2
                    ◇ 9 7 3 2
                    ♣ A 7 4
    ♠ A 8 7 6 2                    ♠ —
    ♡ A K 7 3                      ♡ Q J 9 6
    ◇ J 5                          ◇ Q 10 8 6 4
    ♣ 9 3                          ♣ J 10 8 5
                    ♠ K J 10 9 5 3
                    ♡ 4
                    ◇ A K
                    ♣ K Q 6 2
```

If East is allowed to win the third round of clubs, he has no way of preventing you from ruffing your fourth club in dummy. West can, of course, step in with a trump on the third round of clubs and play the ace and another trump, but then you can simply draw trumps and cash your winning queen of clubs.

Note the importance of ruffing a heart when you are in dummy with the ace of clubs. If you don't make sure of scoring a trick with the five of spades at this stage you will never do so. West will discard a heart on the third round of clubs and a further heart when you ruff East's diamond return high. His trump holding will then be worth two tricks.

♠ 5
♡ A J 6 5
◇ J 8 3 2
♣ K 10 8 3

♠ A 6
♡ 10 9 7 2
◇ A K Q 5
♣ Q 7 6

E–W game.
Dealer North.

West	North	East	South
—	pass	pass	4♠
pass	pass	pass	

You start with two rounds of diamonds, East following with the four and the nine, South with the six and the ten. How should you continue?

From partner's low–high signal you know that declarer has no more diamonds. But why did East play the nine rather than the seven of diamonds on the second round? It must be intended as a suit-preference signal indicating that his values lie in hearts and not in clubs. Partner is suggesting a heart switch, but a suggestion is not a command and it would be as well to look closely at the position before deciding on your continuation.

Declarer apparently has the ace of clubs and he will no doubt have seven good spades, solid apart from the ace, which gives him nine tricks. Where can he hope to find a tenth? From clubs, perhaps, if he has the jack and takes the right view to catch your queen. But South can have no more than four cards in hearts and clubs. A heart switch will be necessary at this point only if he has a doubleton heart and A J in clubs.

If South has a singleton heart, however, a heart switch will be highly dangerous, for South may make his contract on a double squeeze even if he lacks the jack of clubs. On balance it seems probable that East will have four hearts rather than three in view of his signal.

There is only one way to counter the threat of the double

squeeze. You must wipe out the diamond menace in dummy. Continue with the queen of diamonds at trick three, win the ace of trumps on the first round, and play your fourth diamond while partner can still ruff. Then you can hang on to your clubs while partner looks after the hearts in the ending.

The complete deal:

```
                    ♠ 5
                    ♡ A J 6 5
                    ◇ J 8 3 2
                    ♣ K 10 8 3
   ♠ A 6                           ♠ 8 4 3
   ♡ 10 9 7 2                      ♡ K Q 8 3
   ◇ A K Q 5                       ◇ 9 7 4
   ♣ Q 7 6                         ♣ J 5 2
                    ♠ K Q J 10 9 7 2
                    ♡ 4
                    ◇ 10 6
                    ♣ A 9 4
```

You see what would happen on a heart switch? South would win, knock out your ace of spades, ruff the next heart and run his trumps to produce this ending:

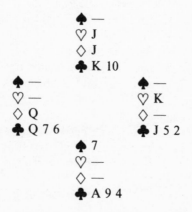

```
                    ♠ —
                    ♡ J
                    ◇ J
                    ♣ K 10
   ♠ —                             ♠ —
   ♡ —                             ♡ K
   ◇ Q                             ◇ —
   ♣ Q 7 6                         ♣ J 5 2
                    ♠ 7
                    ♡ —
                    ◇ —
                    ♣ A 9 4
```

On the last trump you would have to part with a club. The diamond jack would be thrown from dummy and the pressure would be too great for East.

        ♠ Q 7
        ♡ K Q J 8 5 4
        ◇ 9
        ♣ K Q 6 5

♠ A 10
♡ A 10 3 2
◇ A K Q   Game all.
♣ J 9 8 3   Dealer East.

West	*North*	*East*	*South*
—	—	pass	2◇*
dble	2NT	pass	3♠
pass	pass	pass	

* Multi, in this case a weak two in spades, 6–10 points.

On your lead of the ace of diamonds partner plays the ten and declarer the two. How do you continue?

Partner's signal indicates that he holds an even number of diamonds and denies possession of the jack. So you know that declarer started with three diamonds headed by the jack. Declarer is marked with the ace of clubs, of course, and also with the king of spades. In theory South could muster six high-card points with the jack of spades instead of the king, but in practice he would not make a vulnerable two bid with such a weak suit. Just about the only asset that you can hope to find in partner's hand is the jack of spades.

It looks as though you ought to be able to put together five tricks for the defence, but it is hard to see exactly how. Suppose you adopt the obvious defence of playing the ace and another spade. Declarer will win in dummy, cross to hand with the ace of clubs, cash the spade king and continue with three more spades. Unable to part with a club, you will have to let a winning diamond go. And as soon as you do that, declarer will play a heart to set up his ninth trick.

A defence that may work is to switch to the ace and another heart. If partner can ruff the second heart, he will return a diamond to force dummy to ruff. Then a further heart lead when you are in with the ace of spades will enable partner to apply the uppercut with the spade jack. Unfortunately this defence will be disastrous if it is declarer who has the singleton heart.

There is only one defence that will work against all distributions, provided that partner has the vital jack of spades. You should cash the ace of spades at trick two and then switch back to diamonds. Then you can be sure of scoring two trumps, the ace of hearts and two diamonds.

The complete deal:

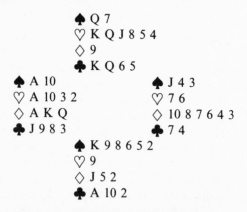

```
              ♠ Q 7
              ♡ K Q J 8 5 4
              ◇ 9
              ♣ K Q 6 5
♠ A 10                      ♠ J 4 3
♡ A 10 3 2                  ♡ 7 6
◇ A K Q                     ◇ 10 8 7 6 4 3
♣ J 9 8 3                   ♣ 7 4
              ♠ K 9 8 6 5 2
              ♡ 9
              ◇ J 5 2
              ♣ A 10 2
```

This deal comes from the match between Britain and Denmark in the 1979 European Championships at Lausanne. At the table the winning defence was not found.

The Multi 2 ◇ opening can certainly create problems for the

defenders. The next example comes from the Caransa Tournament of 1978.

```
                          ♠ J 10 9 7 2
                          ♡ Q 4
                          ◇ A K Q 7
                          ♣ K 5
                                        ♠ K 6 4 3
                                        ♡ J 8 3
Game all.                               ◇ 8 5
Dealer South.                           ♣ A 8 4 3
```

South	West	North	East
2◇*	pass	2NT†	pass
3♡‡	pass	4♡	pass
pass	pass		

* Multi †forcing enquiry ‡ weak two in hearts

West leads the ten of clubs to the five, ace and seven. How should you continue?

Partner will need to have something in spades if you are to defeat this contract. You must hope to score two spade tricks and a trump or, alternatively, one spade and two trumps. A spade switch at trick two will be the right defence if partner has the doubleton ace of spades and doubleton ten of hearts, for the third round of spades will promote a trump trick.

The other possibility is that partner has something like queen doubleton in spades and A 10 or K 10 in trumps. In that case a diamond switch may well enable you to score a diamond ruff as the setting trick.

Which is more likely, that South's six-card suit is headed by the two top honours, or that he has one top honour in trumps along with an outside ace? It is very hard to say.

In practice East switched to a low spade at trick two. That was the wrong defence, for the complete deal turned out to be:

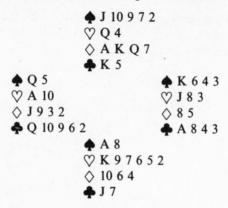

♠ J 10 9 7 2
♡ Q 4
◊ A K Q 7
♣ K 5

♠ Q 5   ♠ K 6 4 3
♡ A 10   ♡ J 8 3
◊ J 9 3 2   ◊ 8 5
♣ Q 10 9 6 2   ♣ A 8 4 3

♠ A 8
♡ K 9 7 6 5 2
◊ 10 6 4
♣ J 7

The wrong defence worked in the event, because declarer made the mistake of winning the spade switch with his ace. When he led a small heart at the next trick West shot up with the ace and played the queen of spades. East overtook with the king and played a third spade, and the defenders could not be denied a second trump trick.

Declarer would have been safe if he had allowed West's queen to win the first round of spades. This would have cut the link between the defenders' hands and no trump promotion would have been possible.

The contract is always defeated by a diamond switch at trick two, however. West plays high enough to force dummy to win, and declarer is in a bit of a quandary. He cannot tackle trumps from dummy without losing two trump tricks and a spade. Nor can he play a spade to his ace without running into the trump promotion. The best he can do is to run the jack of spades to West's queen. Now a further diamond lead from West prepares the way for a ruff on the next round.

For the final example in the chapter we shall look at all four hands from the start. The deal comes from a high-stake rubber game and the contract was played by John Collings, one of the great card-readers of all time.

```
                    ♠ A 10 9 8 7
                    ♡ —
                    ◇ A K 4 2
                    ♣ A K 10 5
    ♠ 6 3                          ♠ Q J
    ♡ J 10 9 8 7                   ♡ A K Q
    ◇ Q 6 5 3                      ◇ 10 9 8
    ♣ J 4                          ♣ Q 9 8 7 6
                    ♠ K 5 4 2
                    ♡ 6 5 4 3 2
Game all.           ◇ J 7
Dealer East.        ♣ 3 2
```

West	North	East	South
—	—	1♣	pass
1♡	dble	2♡	2♠
pass	4♡	dble	pass
pass	5♣	pass	5♠
pass	6◇	pass	6♠
pass	pass	pass	

Once Collings had volunteered a bid of two spades his partner refused to let him off the hook until they were at the six level.

West led the three of spades and declarer went up with dummy's ace, realizing that he needed to find the trumps 2–2. Even then, there appeared to be only eleven tricks. Hoping to find out a little more about the hand, Collings cashed the ace of clubs on which East played the nine and West the four. A second trump was then played to the king and a heart was ruffed in dummy, the fall of the queen from East being duly noted.

Since East had shown up with both spade honours and apparently had the three top hearts, Collings was sure by this time that West must hold the queen of diamonds. West should also have an honour in clubs to justify his response to the opening bid. At trick five, therefore, Collings played the five of clubs from dummy, catching West in an end play of sorts. West naturally chose to return a heart rather than a diamond, but this helped declarer to balance his trumps for the squeeze ending. The heart was ruffed on the table and the king of clubs was cashed, South discarding a diamond and West a heart. This was the position:

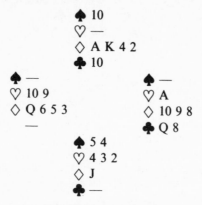

When the ten of clubs was ruffed in the South hand, West was faced with an insoluble problem. No matter which of the red suits he chose to weaken, declarer could ruff it out and make the rest of the tricks.

West might have tried to save the day by dropping the jack of clubs under the ace at trick two, but this would not have posed much of a problem for a declarer like Collings. South would simply have changed direction to end-play East. After a spade to the king and a heart ruff, he would have cashed the top diamonds, ruffed a diamond in hand and ruffed another heart in dummy. This would have been the position:

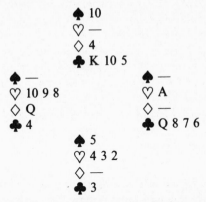

♠ 10
♡ —
◇ 4
♣ K 10 5

♠ —
♡ 10 9 8
◇ Q
♣ 4

♠ —
♡ A
◇ —
♣ Q 8 7 6

♠ 5
♡ 4 3 2
◇ —
♣ 3

If East keeps the ace of hearts when the fourth diamond is ruffed, he is thrown in with it at the next trick. If East jettisons the ace of hearts, a club is ducked into his hand.

Chapter 8

THE LOGIC OF DISTRIBUTION

Bridge is not really a mathematical game and, as we noted earlier, there are few mathematicians among the top-ranking players. Nevertheless, the way in which the fifty-two cards of the pack are distributed between the four players is controlled by strict mathematical laws, and every expert has some awareness, whether instinctive or cultivated, of the manner in which these laws operate.

This is not to say that the mind of the expert is needlessly cluttered with a mass of probability figures. Like all competent players the expert will have memorized rough figures for the common suit breaks. He will know that when four cards are missing they will be divided 3–1 half the time and 2–2 40 per cent of the time, and that when five cards are missing the odds on the 3–2 and 4–1 breaks are about 68 per cent and 28 per cent respectively. When six cards are missing he will be aware that there is only a 36 per cent chance of finding a 3–3 split, against 48 per cent for 4–2 and 15 per cent for 5–1. He may even know that with seven cards missing the chances of the 4–3 and 5–2 breaks are 62 per cent and 31 per cent. But that is likely to be the limit of what he carries in his memory in the way of probability figures. It is quite enough.

These figures can act as useful guides in many situations, but the expert avoids the mistake of attaching too much importance to them. He knows that the odds do not remain static during the play of a hand but are constantly modified as new information comes to light. The trick is knowing how to apply the modified odds in practical play.

Most players would go along with the declarer's line of play on this hand.

```
              ♠ 3
              ♡ 9 6 5 3
              ◇ A K 9 8 4
              ♣ J 8 4

              ♠ A K 6
              ♡ A K 4
Game all.     ◇ 7 3 2
Dealer South. ♣ A 10 9 6
```

South	West	North	East
1♣	pass	1◇	pass
2NT	pass	3NT	pass
pass	pass		

West led the jack of spades and East encouraged with the eight. South won with the king and surveyed his prospects, which seemed quite reasonable. With seven top tricks he needed to develop just two extra tricks in one of the minor suits.

At trick two South played a diamond to dummy's king, West following with the five and East with the six. Then he led the eight of clubs and ran it to West's king. South won the spade return, crossed to the ace of diamonds and led the jack of clubs. He was now in a position to score three club tricks if East had the queen. Unfortunately West produced the queen, and the defenders promptly cashed three spade tricks to put the contract one down.

The complete deal:

'You'd have made it if you had ducked a diamond,' North pointed out.

'Clever of you to spot it,' snarled South. 'That play would have been against the odds. There was a 76 per cent chance of finding at least one of the club honours with East, and only a 68 per cent chance of a 3–2 diamond break.'

This display of erudition was enough to silence North, and South remained in ignorance of the fact that it was *he* who had gone against the odds. Superficially he was correct in his claim that the probability of a 3–2 diamond break was 68 per cent, but that is the *a priori* probability, calculated before the deal and before anything is known about the hand. Once both defenders have followed with small cards to a round of diamonds the whole position changes. Certain distributions can be ruled out as impossible, and the ratio of the probabilities of those that remain can be expressed in a new percentage figure. The 5–0 diamond break is disproved, for example, and three of the five possible 4–1 breaks are also ruled out—those cases where the singleton is an honour card. Four of the ten 3–2 cases are also eliminated—where a defender has Q J, Q 10, J 10, or Q J 10, and we are left with a rough ratio of 41 (three-fifths of 68) to 11 (two-fifths of 28) in favour of the 3–2 break. This gives a theoretical probability of over 78 per cent. In practice the probability is nearer 90 per cent, for it is unlikely that West, with Q J 10 5, would fail to split his honours. Furthermore, if East held Q J 10 6 it would cost him nothing to drop an honour on the first round in the hope of misleading you.

So the expert play, which would duly have landed the contract, is to duck a diamond at trick three.

More important than the memorizing of tables is an appreciation of the amount of space available in the enemy hands. The structure of the game imposes a limit of thirteen cards in the hand of each player. If one player is known to have length in a particular suit there is less space in his hand for cards in the other suits, and this can have a dramatic effect on the odds. The expert will often go out of his way to discover how one suit is breaking before tackling another. Here is an example:

♠ Q
♡ K Q 8 4 2
♢ Q J 9 7 4
♣ Q 5

♠ A K J 4
♡ A 10 6 3
♢ A 6
♣ K J 7

N–S game.
Dealer North.

West	North	East	South
—	1♡	pass	2♣
pass	3♢	pass	3♡
pass	4♡	pass	4NT
pass	5♣	pass	6NT
pass	pass	pass	

Your idea in bidding the slam in notrumps was to protect your king of clubs, but when West leads the ten of spades and dummy goes down you see that it is the diamond position that needed protection from the opening lead. Anyway, you are in the best contract and the queen of spades wins the first trick. How should you continue?

Twelve tricks are available as long as you do not lose a heart, and the heart spots are such that you can cope with a void in either defender's hand. The manner in which you tackle the suit may be crucial, however. If you start with a high heart from dummy you will have to lose a trick when East is void, while if you begin with a low heart to your ace you will lose out when West is void. Which method do you choose?

The answer should be neither—until you know a little more about the hand. The way to find out how the hearts are likely to lie is to investigate the black suits, and you should start by playing the queen of clubs at trick two. If this is allowed to win, continue with a second club. To be sure, it will be awkward if East wins the second club and shoots back a diamond. That will remove a vital entry from your hand, and you will be unable to cope with a heart void in the East hand (unless you risk a first round finesse). In practice it is West who wins the second club, for the complete deal is as follows:

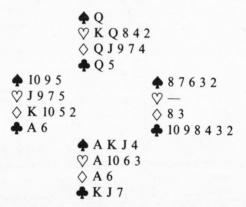

```
            ♠ Q
            ♡ K Q 8 4 2
            ◇ Q J 9 7 4
            ♣ Q 5
♠ 10 9 5                    ♠ 8 7 6 3 2
♡ J 9 7 5                   ♡ —
◇ K 10 5 2                  ◇ 8 3
♣ A 6                       ♣ 10 9 8 4 3 2
            ♠ A K J 4
            ♡ A 10 6 3
            ◇ A 6
            ♣ K J 7
```

When West takes the second club and plays a second spade, you continue with two more spades, noting West's discard of a diamond on the fourth round. When you cash the third club West parts with another diamond. Now all is revealed. East began with eleven cards in the black suits and he is the only one who may be void in hearts. Accordingly you tackle the hearts by cashing the ace first. When East shows out, you continue with the ten of hearts to the jack and queen, return to the ace of diamonds, and take a further heart finesse to bring home your slam.

Suppose that, instead of leading a spade, West begins with the ace and another club. Now it is impossible to disentangle the blocked spades without using up your side entry in diamonds. The best you can do is to win the second club in hand and continue with a third round. When West shows out you have the indication you need. It is no longer a certainty, but there is a valid inference that East, with six clubs, is more likely to be void in hearts than West, who has only two clubs. You should therefore play the ace of hearts at trick four.

Evidence of length in one suit makes it possible to calculate the probable location of a key card in another.

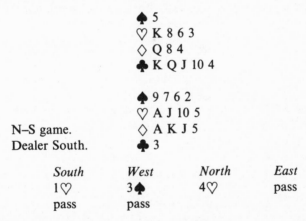

```
              ♠ 5
              ♡ K 8 6 3
              ◇ Q 8 4
              ♣ K Q J 10 4

              ♠ 9 7 6 2
              ♡ A J 10 5
N–S game.     ◇ A K J 5
Dealer South. ♣ 3
```

	South	West	North	East
	1♡	3♠	4♡	pass
	pass	pass		

West leads the ace of spades and East drops the king. On the continuation of the queen of spades you try the eight of hearts from dummy, but East overruffs with the nine of hearts and returns a diamond to your ace. You play the five of hearts to dummy's king, West following with the four and East with the two. When you continue with the three of hearts from the table East produces the seven. Do you finesse or play the ace?

Take your time, for it will cost you the contract if you do the wrong thing here. You have to compare the probability of West holding the singleton four of trumps with that of his having Q 4. A glance at the probability table, if you happen to have one handy, tells you that the doubleton is more likely in the ratio of 6 to 5. But the *a priori* probabilities are irrelevant here for a great deal is already known about the distribution.

The expert way of arriving at the odds in situations like this is to count vacant places. The distribution of the spade suit is known and all the small hearts have been seen, so both these suits can be admitted to the calculation. West is known to have started with seven spades and one small heart, which leaves five vacant places in his hand. East has produced one spade and three small hearts, leaving nine vacant places where the queen of hearts may be hiding. The odds are therefore nine to five that the queen of hearts is with East, and you should take the finesse in the expectation that the complete deal looks something like this:

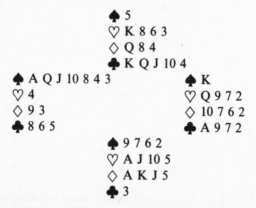

This sort of calculation is very simple to make at the table. Note that it does not yield a rough and ready answer but gives the precise odds at the moment of decision.

You have to follow the rules, however. Suits may be included in the calculation only when the complete distribution is known, although the critical suit may be included when the location of all the small cards is known. In the last example you had seen a diamond from each defender, but it would have been wrong to include these cards in the calculation since the full distribution of the diamond suit was unknown.

The count of vacant places will give you the right answer time after time, but there is one trap which every expert has learned to watch out for. In certain well-defined situations the odds have to be adjusted to take account of what is known as 'the probability of cause'. These situations arise when a defender, in winning a trick or following suit, has a free choice between two cards which he knows to be equals—two adjacent honour cards, for instance. There is no reason to assume that he will prefer one card to the other. Presumably he will play each card about half of the time. When a defender does produce such a card, therefore, the probability that he has both cards has to be halved. An example will perhaps help to make this clear.

$\spadesuit$ K 4
$\heartsuit$ 9 6 5 2
$\diamondsuit$ K 7 5
$\clubsuit$ A K 8 3

$\spadesuit$ Q J 2
$\heartsuit$ A K 10 8 3
$\diamondsuit$ 8 2
$\clubsuit$ Q 7 2

Love all.
Dealer North.

West	North	East	South
—	1$\clubsuit$	1$\diamondsuit$	1$\heartsuit$
pass	2$\heartsuit$	pass	4$\heartsuit$
pass	pass	pass	

West leads the jack of diamonds and continues with a diamond to his partner's queen. You ruff the third round with the eight of hearts and West, to your relief, follows suit. When you cash the ace of hearts West plays the jack and East the four. You cross to the king of clubs and play another heart from the table, East contributing the seven. Do you finesse or play for the drop?

Such problems have to be tackled in two stages. First you go through the usual motions of counting vacant places. The count of the diamond suit is not absolute but, having regard to the bidding, it is a safe working assumption that West began with three and East with five. All the small hearts have been located, West having played one heart and East two. That leaves West with nine vacant places to East's six, and the odds would appear to be three to two on the queen of hearts being in the West hand.

But there is still an adjustment to be made. Remember that you are comparing the probability of West holding the singleton jack of hearts with that of his having Q J doubleton. With the bare jack West would have no option but to play it on the first round of the suit, but with both queen and jack he would have a free choice between equals. He would choose to play the jack only half of the time, and therefore only half the probability of this holding can be counted.

The effect is to reverse the whole position. From being the outsider at 3 to 2 against, East becomes the favourite to hold the queen of hearts at 4 to 3 on. The percentage play is to take the finesse, playing for the full hand to be something like:

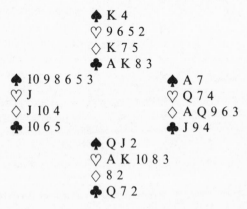

     ♠ K 4
     ♡ 9 6 5 2
     ◇ K 7 5
     ♣ A K 8 3

♠ 10 9 8 6 5 3   ♠ A 7
♡ J   ♡ Q 7 4
◇ J 10 4   ◇ A Q 9 6 3
♣ 10 6 5   ♣ J 9 4

     ♠ Q J 2
     ♡ A K 10 8 3
     ◇ 8 2
     ♣ Q 7 2

The expert's big advantage in dealing with questions of probability is his aptitude for seeing the problems of each hand as a whole. Projecting the play forward in his mind, he is able to visualize the pitfalls that lie ahead. And he remains aware at all times of the fact that the correct percentage play in a particular suit may not represent the best chance of success for the contract.

Here is a deceptive example.

```
                   ♠ 10 3
                   ♡ 7 6 3
                   ◇ A J 10 8 4
                   ♣ 6 4 3


                   ♠ A Q J 5
                   ♡ A K 2
Game all.          ◇ K 6 5
Dealer South.      ♣ A K Q
```

South	West	North	East
2♣	pass	2◇	pass
3NT	pass	4NT	pass
6NT	pass	pass	pass

West leads the ten of clubs against your slam. How do you plan the play?

Four diamond tricks and three spade tricks will see you home, and it looks at first glance as though you just need to find one of the two finesses right. The best chance of avoiding a diamond loser is to cash the king first and then finesse the ten on the second round. That guarantees at least four diamond tricks without loss whenever West has the queen and also when East has the queen singleton.

But the situation is not quite so simple as that because you will have a communication problem when the diamond finesse loses. Suppose that East wins the second diamond and returns a club or a heart. You can enter dummy in diamonds and discard the losing heart on the fourth diamond, but when you cash the last diamond you have an embarrassing discard to make. The South hand is in fact squeezed in spades. Whether you discard the low spade or an honour from your hand, you will not be able to enjoy three spade tricks unless East began with the king singleton or doubleton.

In surveying his prospects the expert is likely to see this trouble looming ahead and to realize that the spade finesse must be taken before the diamonds are run. Accordingly, he will play a low diamond to dummy's ten at trick two, giving up a small part of his chances in the diamond suit for the sake of an extra entry to dummy. His foresight pays off when the complete deal turns out to be something like this:

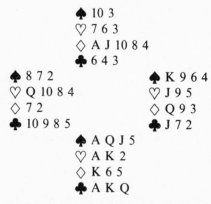

```
              ♠ 10 3
              ♡ 7 6 3
              ◇ A J 10 8 4
              ♣ 6 4 3
   ♠ 8 7 2                    ♠ K 9 6 4
   ♡ Q 10 8 4                 ♡ J 9 5
   ◇ 7 2                      ◇ Q 9 3
   ♣ 10 9 8 5                 ♣ J 7 2
              ♠ A Q J 5
              ♡ A K 2
              ◇ K 6 5
              ♣ A K Q
```

The diamond finesse loses to the queen, and after winning the club return South continues with the king of diamonds. When West follows with a diamond it is safe for declarer to overtake with dummy's ace, for if East shows out there will be a marked finesse against the nine of diamonds on the third round. Both defenders follow to the second diamond, as it happens, and the ten of spades is now led for a finesse. Whether East covers or not, South cannot be denied the three spade tricks he needs for his contract.

The play of a low diamond to the ten is a full 15 per cent better than the play of the king of diamonds at trick two.

Chapter 9

THE PRAGMATIST IN ACTION

Above all else, the bridge expert is a practical creature. Most of the techniques that he employs are trusted tools that have served him well in the past, but he has a flexible mind and is willing to embrace anything new that he feels is likely to work in practice. He has little respect for theory and will often abandon the 'book' bid or play if he can see an advantage in being unorthodox. The pragmatist is not proud. Anything that increases the chance of making (or defeating) the contract is grist to his mill, and he would as soon succeed by means of an outrageous bluff as by the most artistic technical manoeuvre.

In playing the hand the expert tries for maximum safety while recognizing that safety is a relative matter. He knows that a safety play that guarantees a certain number of tricks in a suit may be hideously unsafe in the context of the complete hand. Where no standard safety play is available, the master falls back on his imagination. Working from first principles, he is often able to improvise a safety play to suit the occasion. Overtricks are shunned (except at match-point pairs) if any risk to the contract is involved.

In defence it is comforting to partner a pragmatist, who can be relied on to take the strain whenever it is possible. If he can see a way of defeating the contract, he will take charge of the defence rather than leave his partner on lead in a guessing situation.

Here is a defensive problem of a type that comes up quite frequently:

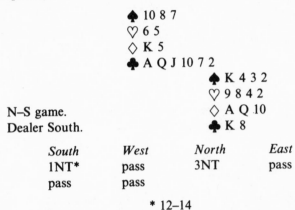

```
                    ♠ 10 8 7
                    ♡ 6 5
                    ◇ K 5
                    ♣ A Q J 10 7 2
                              ♠ K 4 3 2
                              ♡ 9 8 4 2
N–S game.                     ◇ A Q 10
Dealer South.                 ♣ K 8
```

South	West	North	East
1NT*	pass	3NT	pass
pass	pass		

* 12–14

West leads the queen of spades on which you play the four and South the five. Partner's continuation of the six of spades goes to the king and ace, and the nine of clubs is then run to your king. How should you continue?

The position seems quite straightforward, for partner is marked with two more winning spades. You therefore have enough tricks to defeat the contract with the king of clubs, the ace of diamonds and three spades.

It is possible to do better than that, of course. If you return a spade to let partner cash his spade tricks and he then finds the diamond switch, the contract will go two down. How will West know to switch to diamonds instead of hearts? Well, if you had held the ace of hearts you would certainly have cashed it before returning a spade. The fact that you failed to do this implies that you want a diamond return through dummy's king. Partner ought to be able to work it out, and if he doesn't you can always bawl him out afterwards.

But the pragmatist is interested only in defeating the contract—not in bawling out his partner—and he has learned the wisdom of settling for a sure plus score. To avoid all chance of a nasty defensive accident, he cashes the ace of diamonds before returning a spade.

The complete deal:

♠ 10 8 7
♡ 6 5
◇ K 5
♣ A Q J 10 7 2

♠ Q J 9 6   ♠ K 4 3 2
♡ J 10 7 3   ♡ 9 8 4 2
◇ 8 7 6 4   ◇ A Q 10
♣ 3   ♣ K 8

♠ A 5
♡ A K Q
◇ J 9 3 2
♣ 9 6 5 4

In a pairs tournament there would be a much stronger case for returning a spade at trick four and hoping for partner to find the diamond switch. That would certainly be the right play if you were desperate for tops. But if all you needed to do was to avoid bottoms, there would still be something to be said for cashing the ace of diamonds before returning a spade. After all, partner might have led a heart originally, which would have given declarer nine easy tricks.

Take the declarer's seat for the next hand.

♠ A Q J
♥ A K 7 5 4
♦ A 3
♣ 9 7 3

♠ K 5 2
♥ 6 2
♦ K 10 8 7 4 2
♣ A K

Game all.
Dealer South.

South	West	North	East
1◇	pass	2♡	pass
2NT	pass	4NT	pass
6NT	pass	pass	pass

West leads the eight of spades against your slam. How do you plan the play?

North just about has the values for his bidding but it is a pity that there is so much wastage in the spade department, with ten high-card points providing only three tricks. Your chances would have been rosier if one of the minor spade honours had been in diamonds instead.

Still, it is a good slam and the prospects are far from dim. Five diamond tricks along with three spades, two hearts and two clubs will see you home. There will be no problem if the diamonds divide 3–2. What about a 4–1 break?

You will have no chance if one defender has a small singleton and his partner Q J 9 x. If West has a high singleton, the queen, jack or nine, you can succeed. Once the ace of diamonds has dropped West's card, you can finesse against East on the next round and hold your losers to one trick.

Suppose that it is East who has the singleton? Now a singleton honour card is of no use to you. The only hope is that the singleton is the nine, in which case it can be pinned by a first-round lead of the ten of diamonds from hand.

The correct line of play is becoming clear. You must win the first trick in hand with the king of spades and play the ten of diamonds, running it if West plays low.

The complete deal:

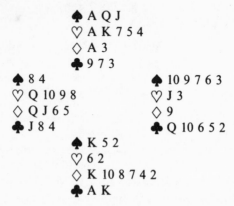

As the cards lie, East's nine of diamonds is pinned and you lose only one trick in the suit whether West covers the ten or not.

Note that you lose none of your other chances by tackling the suit in this manner. If West plays the queen, jack or nine on the first round of diamonds, you go up with dummy's ace and finesse on the way back, forcing East to split his equals if he has the rest of the cards in the suit.

Unorthodox manoeuvres are sometimes needed to achieve complete safety. Here is an example:

♠ A 10 6 5
♡ —
◇ 8 5 3
♣ A K J 10 7 4

♠ K J 9 3
♡ 9 7 6 2
◇ A K 7
♣ Q 3

N–S game.
Dealer North.

West	North	East	South
—	1♣	1♡	1♠
2♡	4♡	pass	6♠
pass	pass	pass	

West leads the ace of hearts which you ruff on the table. It is an excellent slam, for you can afford to give up a trump and still come to twelve tricks. On this forcing heart lead, however, there is some slight danger of losing control. You must arrange to give up your trump trick while there are still trumps in dummy to take care of a heart return. At trick two you lead the six of spades from the table, and when East plays the four you finesse the nine. This wins the trick as West follows with the two of spades. How should you continue?

The obvious move is to play a second trump to the ace and repeat the finesse on the way back. Even if East started with four spades, this line of play should bring in all thirteen tricks.

No doubt you would make thirteen tricks nine times out of ten, but the trouble with this line of play is that it is not completely safe. For there is no guarantee that it is not West who started with four spades! It would be correct defence for West, holding four spades, to allow your nine to win (to take his queen would make things easy for you). If West *does* have the rest of the spades, you will lose control and crash to defeat if you play the ace of spades on the next round.

The way to guard against this eventuality is very simple once you think of it. Having finessed in trumps against East, you must now take a trump finesse against West. Lead the three of spades and insert dummy's ten if West follows with a low trump. East is welcome to score the queen of spades if he has it, for the ace of trumps remains in dummy to take care of a heart return.

This is the distribution you are protecting against:

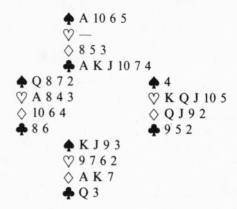

Ducking the first trump was a good effort by West, but as it happens it enables you to make all thirteen tricks. When the finesse of the ten of spades wins and East shows out, you just cash the ace of spades, return to hand with a top diamond, draw West's last trump and claim the remainder.

When the decision is close between taking a finesse and playing for the drop, the pragmatist takes account of any extra chances that may be available.

♠ 4 3 2
♡ K J 8 4 3
◇ 4
♣ Q 9 8 6

♠ A 10
♡ A 10 7 5
◇ A K J 6
♣ K 4 2

Love all.
Dealer South.

South	West	North	East
1♡	1♠	2♡	2♠
3NT	pass	4♡	pass
pass	pass		

West leads the king of spades which you allow to win the first trick, and the spade continuation goes to your ace. How do you plan the play?

The prospects for game are fairly good, although a misguess in trumps will mean that you can afford to lose only one club trick. If anyone is short in trumps it is likely to be West, so there is a case for taking a second-round finesse through East. It is a fairly close decision, however.

What about extra chances? If you play for the drop unsuccessfully you can always fall back on the diamond finesse, hoping to discard two club losers from dummy. If you intend to follow this line you will need to win the second round of trumps in dummy. But the prospects are rather better if you take a losing trump finesse, provided that you do a little elimination first.

The best line of play is to cash the ace of diamonds, ruff the small diamond in dummy and ruff the third spade in your hand. Then play a trump to dummy's king and a trump back for a finesse of the ten. If West wins with a doubleton queen, he will either have to lead a diamond or open up the clubs, probably to your advantage.

The complete deal:

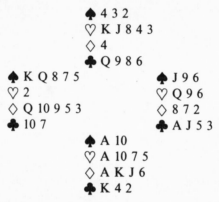

As it happens your problems are solved when the heart finesse wins. But if West had held the doubleton queen of hearts he would have been end-played. A spade or a diamond return would give you the contract immediately, and the best West could do would be to return the ten of clubs. Then you would just have to read the club position correctly, covering with dummy's queen, to make the contract.

The handling of trumps in defence can pose interesting problems. Take the West seat for the next hand.

```
              ♠ Q J 4
              ♡ 3
              ◇ K 7 6 4
              ♣ A Q J 8 5
♠ A 6
♡ 5
◇ J 9 8 5 3 2                              N–S game.
♣ 9 7 4 3                                  Dealer North.
```

West	North	East	South
—	1♣	1♡	dble
2◇	pass	pass	2♠
pass	3♠	pass	4♠
pass	pass	pass	

On your lead of the five of hearts East plays the ace and South the seven. Partner returns the nine of hearts to declarer's ten. How do you plan the defence?

That nine of hearts looks very like a suit-preference signal asking for a diamond return. Assuming that partner has the ace of diamonds and that it will stand up, you have three aces to cash. A fourth defensive trick can come only from trumps. Your six of spades can possibly be used to uppercut dummy, forcing out a high trump and perhaps promoting an intermediate trump in your partner's hand.

But the uppercut must not be attempted too early. In order to get the timing right you must first step out of the way with the ace of spades. Ruff with the spade ace at trick two, return the nine of diamonds to partner's ace, and apply the uppercut with the six of spades on the next heart.

You are hoping for the complete deal to be something like the following:

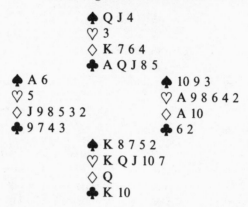

```
                    ♠ Q J 4
                    ♡ 3
                    ◇ K 7 6 4
                    ♣ A Q J 8 5
    ♠ A 6                         ♠ 10 9 3
    ♡ 5                           ♡ A 9 8 6 4 2
    ◇ J 9 8 5 3 2                 ◇ A 10
    ♣ 9 7 4 3                     ♣ 6 2
                    ♠ K 8 7 5 2
                    ♡ K Q J 10 7
                    ◇ Q
                    ♣ K 10
```

Note that it is not good enough to ruff with the six of spades at trick two. Declarer can overruff on the table, enter his hand with a club, and lead a low trump to knock out your ace. The ace of diamonds is then the only other trick for the defence.

In defence it is particularly important to give declarer nothing that is not his for the taking anyway. Often this boils down to the routine chore of counting declarer's tricks.

```
                    ♠ 10 9 2
                    ♡ J 10 9 7 2
                    ◇ A 9
                    ♣ 9 6 4
                              ♠ J 6
                              ♡ 5
E–W game.                     ◇ K 7 5 4 2
Dealer South.                 ♣ K J 10 8 2
```

South	West	North	East
1♠	2♡	2♠	pass
4♠	pass	pass	pass

West leads the king of hearts, and when dummy goes down you are glad that you were not doubled in two hearts. The profit will be small if the opponents succeed in making four spades, however. South follows to the first trick with the four of hearts, and West continues with the heart three. You ruff with the jack of spades and South, after a little thought, overruffs with the king. The three of diamonds is led to West's eight and dummy's ace, and the nine of diamonds is returned. You win with the king as partner drops the jack. How should you continue?

For the defence to have a chance, you must assume that South has no more than five spades and that partner has a trump trick. If South began with three diamonds and four clubs he is destined to lose a trick in each suit. The dangerous situation is where he started with four diamonds and three clubs. Counting declarer's tricks, you see that he has four trump tricks in his hand plus three diamonds, the ace of clubs, and perhaps a club ruff on the table once he has discarded dummy's clubs on his diamonds. It adds up to only nine tricks, and the straightforward defence of returning your trump should therefore defeat him. The one thing you must not do is return a club, which may offer declarer the chance to take a finesse that he cannot conveniently take for himself.

The complete deal:

♠ 10 9 2
♡ J 10 9 7 2
◇ A 9
♣ 9 6 4

♠ Q 7 3
♡ A K Q 8 6 3
◇ J 8
♣ 7 3

♠ J 6
♡ 5
◇ K 7 5 4 2
♣ K J 10 8 2

♠ A K 8 5 4
♡ 4
◇ Q 10 6 3
♣ A Q 5

Do you see what happens if you return a club? South gratefully finesses the queen and plays the queen of diamonds. If West ruffs, dummy overruffs, the South hand is entered with the ace of spades and the ten of diamonds is led. Declarer throws a club from dummy whether West ruffs with his master trump or not, and eventually the losing club is ruffed on the table. It does West no good to discard his second club on the queen of diamonds instead of ruffing. Dummy also discards a club, and the play of the ten of diamonds places West in the same impossible position. Whether West ruffs or not, he cannot prevent the ruff of the losing club in dummy.

The timing is different if East returns a trump, since South has not had the opportunity to finesse in clubs. When South plays the queen of diamonds West can discard a club. South may ruff in dummy in order to take the club finesse, but there is no way for him to dispose of his losing club and the contract must go one down.

As the cards lie, a diamond return from East also serves to defeat the contract. It is only a club switch that is fatal to the defence.

Chapter 10

ABSTRACT BEAUTY

The time has come to take a look at the metaphysical rewards of pure technique. All experts know and value this aspect of the game but none has so far attempted to explain it.

Acquiring bridge skill is a little like climbing a mountain. It may be a hard slog, but each upward step brings increased pleasure as new and delightful vistas are revealed. Beyond the half-way point the view can be quite breath-taking. The clouds disperse briefly and the climber is rewarded by moments of almost unbearable beauty.

To the expert, bridge is an art form. Instead of expressing his personality in the composition of prose or poetry, the application of paint to canvas, or the arrangement of musical notes, the bridge expert does so by the manipulation of card-patterns. All art has been held to be a search for truth and beauty, those elusive qualities that delight the senses, charm the intellect and satisfy the emotions. For seekers after perfection the road is full of pitfalls, but when technique is of the highest order and inspirations flows, the result is sometimes beyond expectations. A well-played bridge hand has as much power to thrill and to satisfy as a Beethoven symphony.

Having experienced one moment of magic, the expert returns again and again to the bridge table hoping to catch a further glimpse of the absolute. His longing is unconnected with his normal motivation for the game, which is ego gratification. Naturally the expert still hopes to find the right path in a difficult situation and often succeeds, but even when he fails he may be enriched and enchanted by the sheer beauty of the hand.

Let me show you a few of the hands in which I have found beauty.

```
              ♠ 10 4
              ♡ K 9 3 2
              ◇ K J 7 4
              ♣ 9 6 3

              ♠ A K 3
              ♡ A Q 10 5
Game all.     ◇ 6 5 3
Dealer South. ♣ A 10 7
```

South	West	North	East
1♡	pass	2♡	2♠
2NT	pass	4♡	pass
pass	pass		

West leads the six of spades and when dummy goes down you see that partner's jump to four hearts was a bit of a stretch. You will need a large slice of luck to bring home this optimistic contract. Dummy's ten of spades is covered by the jack and you win with the ace. Clearly you need to do something with the diamond suit. When you lead the six of diamonds from hand at the second trick, West follows with the two. Which card do you play from dummy?

There is little chance of finding West with both ace and queen of diamonds since it was East who did the bidding. You cannot hope to avoid two diamond losers and you will therefore have to restrict your club losers to one trick. That will be possible only when the clubs are 5–2, for the defenders will surely switch to clubs at the next trick. You will have to win the second club and hope to develop the diamonds without allowing West—presumably the one with the five clubs—to gain the lead.

The above analysis indicates that you cannot afford to play a diamond honour on the first round. You must hope that West has the queen, certainly, but the finesse of the jack must be kept for later. The correct play is a low diamond from dummy.

The complete deal:

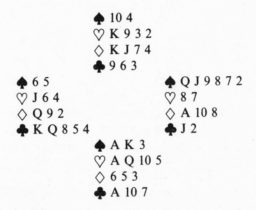

♠ 10 4
♡ K 9 3 2
◇ K J 7 4
♣ 9 6 3

♠ 6 5   ♠ Q J 9 8 7 2
♡ J 6 4   ♡ 8 7
◇ Q 9 2   ◇ A 10 8
♣ K Q 8 5 4   ♣ J 2

♠ A K 3
♡ A Q 10 5
◇ 6 5 3
♣ A 10 7

East wins the first diamond and switches to the jack of clubs. You take the ace of clubs on the second round and play another diamond to the jack and ace. West has no further chance to gain the lead, and eventually your losing club goes away on dummy's fourth diamond.

This line of play still succeeds if West has a diamond more and a heart less, for, after a spade has been ruffed in dummy, West is squeezed on the run of the trumps.

You are not alone if you failed to see the solution. In an international match between England and Scotland the contract went down in both rooms after a diamond to the jack at trick two. The declarers spotted their mistakes immediately and sighed for the pure, austere beauty of that first-round diamond duck.

♠ —
♡ 9 8 6 3
◇ A J 9 6 5 4 3
♣ K 5

♠ A K Q J 8 4
♡ Q J 5

Game all.   ◇ 10
Dealer South.   ♣ A 7 3

	South	*West*	*North*	*East*
	1♠	pass	2◇	pass
	3NT	pass	4◇	pass
	4♠	pass	pass	pass

West leads the four of hearts to his partner's ace. East returns the two of hearts to the king and West continues with a third heart which East ruffs with the five of spades. The four of clubs is then led. How do you plan the play?

What an annoying business! Assuming the spades to be worth six tricks, you would have had a simple task in three notrumps. Perhaps you should think about a change of partner.

Meanwhile you have to try to muster ten tricks in spades and there are only nine on view. A tenth might be established in diamonds if either defender has K Q doubleton, but that is rather unlikely. Alternatively, if West happens to have both diamond honours you will be able to squeeze him in the red suits by running all your black winners. But if that had been the position East might well have switched to a diamond in order to destroy the link with dummy. It is more probable that the diamond honours are divided between the defenders, in which case you must plan to squeeze West in three suits and East in two.

Even if you have never heard of a compound ruffing squeeze, correct technique may see you through. It is essential to win with the ace of clubs at trick four in order to preserve an extra entry in dummy. Then draw four rounds of trumps, discarding diamonds from the table and hoping for the complete deal to be something like this:

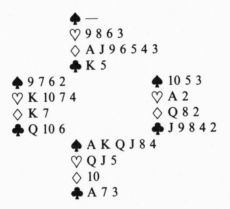

After eight tricks you are down to this five-card end position:

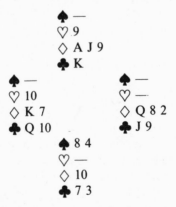

West feels the pressure when you continue with another trump. He cannot afford to throw his heart, and if he lets the seven of diamonds go he exposes his partner to a ruffing finesse in the suit.

West has to part with a club, therefore. You discard the nine of hearts from dummy, and now East is in trouble. If he throws a diamond you can establish your tenth trick in that suit with a ruff. And if he parts with a club, you cross to the king of clubs, cash the ace of diamonds, ruff a diamond, and claim the tenth trick with your seven of clubs.

There is something of the cold, grinding beauty of a glacier in a complex squeeze of this kind. Squeezes inevitably play a starring role in the expert's ideas about beauty. It has something to do with the perfect timing that is required, and with the sense of the proper fitness of things that comes when you have an answer to every move that the defenders may make.

Here is a rather different type of squeeze, and for a change we shall start with all four hands.

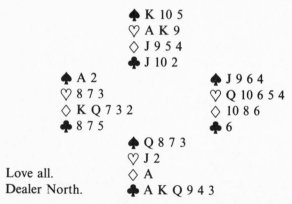

♠ K 10 5
♡ A K 9
♢ J 9 5 4
♣ J 10 2

♠ A 2
♡ 8 7 3
♢ K Q 7 3 2
♣ 8 7 5

♠ J 9 6 4
♡ Q 10 6 5 4
♢ 10 8 6
♣ 6

♠ Q 8 7 3
♡ J 2
♢ A
♣ A K Q 9 4 3

Love all.
Dealer North.

This deal appeared in the annual match between the two Houses of Parliament in 1978. When Sir Timothy Kitson, captain of the Commons team, held the South cards he became declarer in six clubs after West had made an overcall in diamonds.

Winning the opening lead of the king of diamonds, declarer drew three rounds of trumps, noting that West followed three times. Then he led a small spade towards dummy's king. West solved all problems at this point by going up with the ace of spades and trying to cash the queen of diamonds.

If West had played low, declarer intended to win the king of spades and duck a spade on the way back. This would have worked, and although declarer would still have been a trick short he would have been in a position to apply pressure by running his trumps. This would have been the situation when the last trump was led:

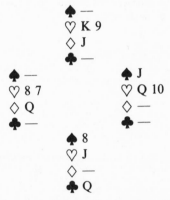

On the play of the queen of clubs West discards a heart, whereupon the jack of diamonds is discarded from dummy and East is caught in a major-suit squeeze.

As the cards lie it is only East who comes under pressure, but the form is that of a double squeeze which would have worked equally well if one or both of the heart honours had been held by West.

It was suggested that an initial heart lead would have been a killer, since West can return another heart when in with the ace of spades, cutting the last link with dummy and destroying all chance of a squeeze.

Not so. The squeeze is a flexible weapon for those who know how to use it. When entries are destroyed in one quarter they may often be found in another. In this case the trump suit can provide the required entries if the proper technique is followed. Here is how the play should develop after a heart lead.

The heart ace wins the first trick, the two of clubs is played to the ace and the ace of diamonds is cashed. Then a spade is led, dummy's king winning the trick when West plays low. A diamond is ruffed in hand and a low spade is played to West's ace. Following his plan, West returns a heart to take out dummy's remaining entry. Declarer ruffs a diamond with the king of clubs, leads a low club to dummy's ten, and ruffs the jack of diamonds with the queen of clubs.

Here is the end position:

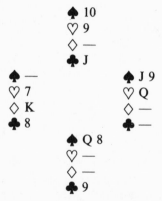

When declarer draws the last trump by entering dummy with the jack of clubs it is all over for East.

Now let us see how good you are at recovering from a bidding accident.

♠ —
♡ A K 4
◇ A K 9 6 4
♣ K 8 7 5 2

♠ 10 8 6 5 3
♡ Q 6 2
◇ 8 7 2
♣ A Q

N–S game.
Dealer West.

West	North	East	South
3♠	4♣	pass	4♡
pass	pass	pass	

Partner's bid of four clubs was for take-out and you had quite a difficult problem. You might have tried four diamonds but you decided on four hearts, taking the view that partner was likely to be well-endowed in the major suit. Whether North should have passed four hearts is an arguable point, but pass he did, leaving you to struggle in a silly game when six diamonds is a fair shot.

West leads the ace of spades. You ruff in dummy with the four of hearts and East follows with the two of spades. How do you plan to score ten tricks?

What do you know about the hand? West opened with a pre-emptive bid of three spades, but he can hardly have seven cards in the suit. With A K Q J x x x his bid would have been four spades, not three spades, at this vulnerability. West must therefore have six spades and East two.

What about the heart position? Assuming that you can score five tricks in the minor suits, you need five tricks from your trumps. In other words, you need to score one of the small trumps in your hand by ruffing. That will be possible only if the trumps break 5–2, for you will have to extract West's trumps before you can safely ruff anything in your hand. Your small trumps are such midgets that West will surely be able to overruff if given the chance. You must therefore ruff only one more spade in dummy, for you need two master trumps to draw those held by West. Precise timing is required.

After ruffing the first trick, you should enter hand with a club, ruff a spade with the king of hearts, then cash the ace of hearts and play a second club to hand. The queen of hearts extracts what you hope is West's last trump, and you continue with two top diamonds. Next you cash the king of clubs, discarding the losing diamond from hand. You need to find East with at least three clubs, of course, and the play to this trick will tell you how to continue. If West shows out, marking East with four clubs, you score your tenth trick by ruffing the fourth round of clubs. If the clubs prove to be 3–3, East is marked with the remaining diamond (West's shape is known to be 6–2–2–3), and you score your tenth trick with a diamond ruff.

The complete deal:

It is really just a matter of taking your ten tricks, isn't it? But the manner of the taking is bound to give you a certain quiet satisfaction, even if they do bid and make six diamonds in the other room.

The next hand comes from a rubber game in America. It was played by Bob Richman, a member of the Australian international team who is American by birth, and was reported in the bulletin of the International Bridge Press Association by Paul Marston of New Zealand, who nominated it as his choice for the best-played hand of 1979.

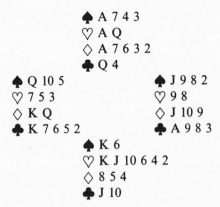

Richman played in four hearts and received a trump lead. There appear to be exactly nine tricks for declarer. Even with all four hands on view it is hard to see how a tenth trick might be made. Although the diamonds can be established to provide extra tricks, the defenders will than have four winners—two in each minor suit.

You might think of ducking a diamond and allowing the defenders to take their club tricks. The timing would then be right for a ruffing squeeze against East in spades and diamonds. No, that will never work, for after cashing their clubs the defenders will surely switch back to diamonds, removing the vital card of entry from dummy.

Without the benefit of seeing all four hands, Richman found the way to make his contract. He played off four rounds of trumps, discarding clubs from dummy and reducing to the following position:

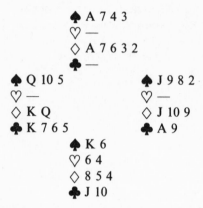

♠ A 7 4 3
♡ —
◇ A 7 6 3 2
♣ —

♠ Q 10 5   ♠ J 9 8 2
♡ —   ♡ —
◇ K Q   ◇ J 10 9
♣ K 7 6 5   ♣ A 9

♠ K 6
♡ 6 4
◇ 8 5 4
♣ J 10

On the next trump West discarded a club and dummy a diamond, and East was in grave difficulty. A spade discard allows declarer to establish dummy's fourth spade with a ruff, and a diamond discard gives up the second stopper in the suit. East might have and probably ought to have discarded the ace of clubs, but as the cards lie this discard would not have helped. Declarer's minor club honours would then have been worth a trick.

In practice East chose to discard the nine of clubs. The defenders were no longer in a position to cash their two club tricks, and Richman took full advantage. He ducked a diamond at the next trick. West won and played a club to his partner's ace, and East returned a spade to the king. Now the play of the ace and another diamond put East back on lead, and declarer's remaining club loser was eventually discarded on the established seven of diamonds.

Instead of ducking a diamond after the fifth trump, declarer might equally well have continued with a sixth round of trumps.

East has to weaken his hand still further, and declarer cannot be denied a tenth trick.

Here is a strange hand that comes from the Budapest heat of the Philip Morris Cup held in January, 1980.

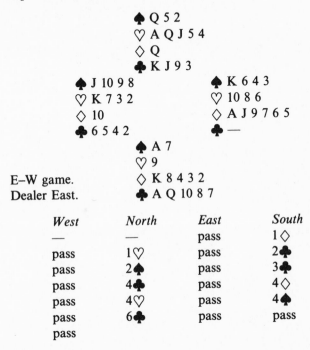

♠ Q 5 2
♡ A Q J 5 4
♢ Q
♣ K J 9 3

♠ J 10 9 8
♡ K 7 3 2
♢ 10
♣ 6 5 4 2

♠ K 6 4 3
♡ 10 8 6
♢ A J 9 7 6 5
♣ —

♠ A 7
♡ 9
♢ K 8 4 3 2
♣ A Q 10 8 7

E–W game.
Dealer East.

West	North	East	South
—	—	pass	1♢
pass	1♡	pass	2♣
pass	2♠	pass	3♣
pass	4♣	pass	4♢
pass	4♡	pass	4♠
pass	6♣	pass	pass
pass			

Six clubs was a popular contract on this deal and the jack of spades was the usual lead. Those declarers who took a direct heart finesse and discarded the spade loser on the heart ace were successful, for after conceding a diamond they were able to crossruff for twelve tricks. Those who tried a ruffing finesse in hearts were unlucky.

The best start for the defence is, in fact, a trump, and the contract was normally defeated when this lead was found. But the well-known Polish international Andrzej Wilkosz made his contract after a trump lead. He won the first trick in hand and played a diamond to the queen and ace. East returned the jack of diamonds, declarer played low, West discarded the eight of spades and dummy ruffed.

At this point declarer paused to take stock. It seemed probable that West had a 4–4–4–1 pattern, and he was unlikely to hold the king of spades since East had not returned that suit. If the eight of spades was a true card West's holding could well be J 10 9 8, in which case it should be possible to establish the seven of spades as a menace against him.

Accordingly, Wilkosz led the queen of spades from the table at trick four. This was covered by the king and ace, a small diamond was ruffed in dummy, the remaining trumps were drawn and the king of diamonds was cashed. The position was now as follows:

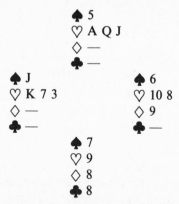

The last trump was led and West was unable to find a good discard. A heart discard would permit South to score three heart tricks by finessing. When in practice West discarded a spade, South cashed the established seven of spades and took the heart finesse to land his slam.

East might have broken up the position by returning a heart

when he in was with the ace of diamonds. This far-sighted defence would certainly have destroyed the major-suit squeeze against West, but it would not necessarily have defeated the contract. If declarer reads the position correctly he can set up a third heart trick by playing on reverse-dummy lines and end up by squeezing East.

The heart return is won in dummy, the ace of hearts is cashed for a diamond discard, and a third heart is ruffed in hand. Dummy is re-entered with the jack of clubs, and a fourth heart is ruffed with the ace of clubs to leave this position:

Declarer overtakes the queen of clubs with dummy's king, draws West's last trump, throwing a diamond from hand, and continues with the queen of hearts. East has to give up his guard in either spades or diamonds, and South simply discards from the other suit and claims the rest of the tricks.

It is rare and satisfying to have a choice of squeezes according to the line adopted by the defence. One final thought. Perhaps the best shot for East when in with the ace of diamonds is to return a spade, putting declarer immediately to the test. If the ace goes up the contract goes down.

If a poll were conducted among the world's top experts to establish which of them is regarded as the best there would be a substantial vote in favour of Benito Garozzo of Italy. Here is a glimpse into the mind of Garozzo which may help to explain why he is held in such high regard.

The deal comes from the final of the 1979 Bermuda Bowl contest between Italy and the USA. In both rooms the contract was three notrumps by South.

♠ Q J 7 3 2
♡ J 10 2
◇ A Q 8
♣ K J

♠ 8 4   ♠ K 10 9 6 5
♡ Q 8 7 3   ♡ A 5
◇ 10 4   ◇ 9 6 5
♣ A 7 6 4 2   ♣ 8 5 3

♠ A
♡ K 9 6 4
◇ K J 7 3 2
♣ Q 10 9

Game all.
Dealer South.

South	West	North	East
De Falco	Eisenberg	Franco	Kantar
1♡	pass	1♠	pass
2◇	pass	3♣	pass
3NT	pass	pass	pass

This was the bidding in the Open Room and West led the four of clubs to dummy's king. De Falco ran the jack of hearts at trick two. Eisenberg won with the queen and continued with the two of clubs, and South was unable to make more than eight tricks.

In a sense it was an unlucky guess by De Falco, who would have made his nine tricks all right if he had put up the king of hearts at trick two. Nevertheless, the general opinion among the cognoscenti in the auditorium was that the hand had been played down. It looks better, after winning the first trick, to play a spade to the ace, return to dummy with a diamond, and continue with the